KU-533-062

A RAILWAY BOOK

FOR BOYS OF ALL AGES

"Away to the West" by "The 10.30 Limited"

A RAILWAY BOOK

FOR BOYS OF ALL AGES

BY W. G. CHAPMAN

PUBLISHED IN 1923 BY

THE GREAT WESTERN RAILWAY

[FELIX J. C. POLE, GENERAL MANAGER]

PADDINGTON STATION, LONDON

Published in Great Britain in 2012 by Old House books & maps,
Midland House, West Way, Botley, Oxford OX2 0PH, United Kingdom.
44-02 23rd Street, Suite 219, Long Island City, NY 11101, USA.
Website: www.oldhousebooks.co.uk

A CIP catalogue record for this book is available from the British Library.

ISBN-13: 978 1 90840 217 2

Originally published in 1923 by the Great Western Railway,
Paddington Station, London.

Printed in China through Worldprint Ltd.

12 13 14 15 16 10 9 8 7 6 5 4 3 2 1

NOTE TO SECOND EDITION.—The gratifying demand for a second edition of this little book within a month of publication affords opportunity for a few slight revisions and additions to the text. A brief description of the new passenger engine "Caerphilly Castle," the prototype of the "Castle" class (4–6–0, 4-cylinder), has been included as its advent marks an epoch in railway locomotive construction. An index has also been added.

September, 1923 *W.G.C.*

A FOREWORD

DESPITE the fascination of aeronautics, wireless telephony, and other wonders of this twentieth century, our railways still hold high place in the esteem and affection of a host of youthful admirers, and for their edification and enlightenment some of the "hows," "whys," and "wherefores" in regard to modern railway practice are here explained.

For the sake of convenience, the explanatory matter has been put into narrative form descriptive of a journey from London to Plymouth by the 10.30 A.M. Cornish Riviera Express. This train has been selected for the reason, among others, that the non-stop run of two hundred and twenty-six miles, which it performs every week-day in the scheduled time of four hours and seven minutes, constitutes a world's record.

It is assumed that the writer and his young reader are making the journey together, and opportunity is taken *en route* to explain and illustrate, in words and pictures, such railway appliances and operations as are of interest to boys of all ages.

In preparing this little volume, the writer has also been influenced by the pressing need that exists for the relief of harassed parents, much-interrogated uncles, and others, who are so frequently called upon to draw from their wells of knowledge in order to satisfy that vast army of embryo railway engineers which is still wearing out its knickerbockers at school. W.G.C.

READING, JUNE 1923

CHAPTERS

WITH 120 ILLUSTRATIONS

CHAPTER THE FIRST

PADDINGTON

THE hands of the big three-faced clock at Paddington Station point to 10.15 as we arrive on Number One platform. There is just time to take a cursory glance at the powerful locomotive which, with its train of twelve coaches, constitutes the most wonderful train in the world, the Cornish Riviera Express, familiarly known as "The 10.30 Limited."

As we pass along the platform we observe the beauty of the "seventy-footer" coaches resplendent in their chocolate and cream, which is the standard colouring of Great Western Railway coaching stock—colours with sweet associations for schoolboys. We notice that vehicles in the rear of the train are labelled for various destinations, and it should be explained that the train includes three portions which are "slipped" *en route*—at Westbury, Taunton, and Exeter respectively—whilst the train is running at high speed. A close examination will shew that the first coach in each slip portion is attached by a special "slip hook," of which more anon when we are on our journey.

It is here interesting to notice that our train carries coaches which are worked through to no fewer than nine different destinations. It is true our Plymouth coach terminates intermediately on the through route, but there are in addition vehicles for Penzance, St. Ives, Falmouth, Kingsbridge, Exeter, Ilfracombe, Minehead, and Weymouth. In the holiday season and at times of traffic pressure it is necessary to redistribute the sections of this train to form two and sometimes three separate trains.* The provision for so many destinations in one train is almost unique in railway practice. The total weight of the train is over 500 tons.

Our engine, " Princess Mary," is a four-cylinder locomotive of the 4-6-0 type. This latter designation is used to represent the wheel arrangement of engines, and in this case signifies that there is a four-wheeled bogie in front, six coupled driving wheels, and no trailing wheels.

Like all Great Western engines, she is painted in black and green, the smoke box and funnel being black and the long graceful boiler green lined out in black, as is also the six-wheeled tender.

On our journey we shall look at some diagrams and photographs of various types of locomotives and have a chat about locomotive operation. Now we have time to do little more than admire the grace and dignity of this " greyhound of the iron track." As we see her this morning, she suggests the embodiment of concentrated power, and appears to be straining at the leash and anxious

* *In the heavy summer service passengers to some of these places are conveyed by other trains and then one slip portion only is taken, i.e. the Westbury slip for Weymouth.*

to stretch herself to full capacity. Driver and firemen are at their posts on the footplate, alert and apparently eager to be off on their four-hour run. They are obviously proud of their charge. Their pride is more than justified with such a powerful and noble example of modern locomotive engineering under their control.

Thanks to the Great Western Railway system of seat * registration, we need have no immediate concern about securing our places in the train, for these are reserved for us. In the few moments which are still available we will take a hasty look at Paddington Station itself. The beautiful arched roof is particularly attractive and forms part of the station as designed by the celebrated engineer Isambard Kingdom Brunel. You may have seen Frith's famous picture " The Railway Station," of which Paddington Station forms the subject. It depicts the architectural engineering as well as the life and pathos of the station in the year 1860 (long before you or I began to

* *Over 10,000 seats have been reserved by registration, in trains leaving Paddington, in a single day.*

take any interest in railways). It is said that twenty-one thousand persons paid to see this work when it was exhibited in London. The original picture is now in Holloway College, Englefield Green, near Egham, where it may be seen by visitors. The station has, of course, been much enlarged since Brunel's day, and now has thirteen platform roads and covers an area of about seventy acres. Incidentally, Paddington was the first railway station to be lighted by electric arc lamps.

Platform Number One is a scene of life and movement. " Hustle without confusion " is, perhaps, a fitting description. Porters are busy with passengers' luggage. Assembled round the carriage doors are friends of passengers "seeing them off." Boys are busy selling choc——I should say, books and newspapers—whilst smartly uniformed inspectors, guards, and porters are looking after the comfort of the travellers in various ways. There is a friendliness about the Great Western Railway, and it is doubtless that old-time courtesy of G.W.R. employees which prompted Sir John Foster Fraser, a traveller familiar with railway stations in both hemispheres, to remark that Paddington Station possessed the most polite staff.

Moving towards our compartment, we pass the imposing War Memorial erected to the honour of the 25,479 Great Western Railwaymen who served with the Colours in the Great War 1914–1918, and to the sacred memory of the 2,524 who were called upon to make the supreme sacrifice. The monument, unique in design, consists of the bronze figure of a soldier standing against a background of marble and granite. Clad in the rough habiliments of war, with greatcoat loosely thrown over his shoulders, he is evidently reading a letter from home.

Although about 150 trains are despatched from Paddington Station and about 160 arrive there on a normal summer day, this is by no means the limit of the station's activities. Approximately 1,500 cabs enter the station daily. Some 4,400 churns of milk arrive and are dealt with during each twenty-four hours, or 1,606,000 churns annually, and the same number of empty churns is despatched. About 42,000 tons of fish arrive at the station in the year; this traffic comes in the early hours of the morning. On a heavy morning as much as 500 tons has been handled. Another perishable seasonal traffic dealt with at Paddington Station is fruit for Covent Garden, the record for one day being 370 tons, representing about 17,500 packages.

Every morning at 2.30 A.M. a special train for the conveyance of newspapers leaves Paddington, with an average load of 2,600 parcels, weighing 42 tons, whilst by other morning trains 3,950 packages of newspapers, having a weight of 55 tons, are despatched: a total of nearly 100 tons of newspapers per day.

Perhaps the most interesting sight is when the Sunday newspaper traffic is handled, and then no fewer than 7,600 packages, weighing 170 tons, are despatched late on Saturday night or early Sunday morning.

This is all apart from the general parcels business, which averages 15,000 packages outwards and 9,500 inwards daily, besides many " boxes " of horses, trucks of scenery for theatrical companies, vans of His Majesty's mails, etc.

There is much of interest to be seen at Paddington Station had we the time to spare, but the hands of the clock are creeping on to the half-hour and we must take our seats in the train.

∽ ∽ ∽ ∽

Carriage doors are now being closed, a green flag is waving in the rear accompanied by a shrill whistle, which is acknowledged by the engine, and then, ever so gently, almost imperceptibly at first, we move out of the station, accompanied by a waving of handkerchiefs and hastily exchanged messages between those on board who are " Going Great Western " and their friends on the platform.

We are off on our two hundred and twenty-six mile non-stop run to Plymouth at 10.30 a.m. to the very tick. Splendid !

CHAPTER THE SECOND

"AWAY TO THE WEST"

YOU take your seat facing the engine. As we leave Paddington Station you will see on your right the electric trains on the Hammersmith & City Railway, which pass by subway under the Great Western lines and emerge just short of Westbourne Park Station. Here we catch a glimpse of Subway Junction Signal Box, and you will be interested to know that during the twenty-four hours of a normal day in the summer upwards of eight hundred and thirty trains and engines pass this box, an average of thirty-five an hour, or one in every minute and three-quarters.

We are now gathering speed. On your right is the Old Oak Common Locomotive and Carriage Depot, where the engines and many of the coaches feeding Paddington Station are stabled and prepared for their journeys. The fine red-brick building which you see at the extreme west end of the yard contains twenty sidings, each one thousand feet long, and is used for the cleaning and equipping of trains. It is here the main line expresses are stabled. Just beyond you will see a line branching off to the north-west. This is the direct and shortest route to Birmingham, and many Great Western express trains make the journey of 110 miles daily in two hours.

At this point you will see another railway passing under the Great Western Railway. This is the Ealing and Shepherds Bush Line, an extension of the Central London Electric Railway from Wood Lane to Ealing, owned by the Great Western Railway. You get another sight of the railway on your right, as we pass Ealing Broadway Station.

You have probably often wondered where some of the well-advertised products, whose names are household words, are manufactured. Just after we pass Southall you will see a large number of modern factories located alongside the railway. Here on the left are the Scott's Emulsion Laboratory and the jam factory of Messrs. Ticklers. On the right are the Gramophone Company's Works, where the familiar sign " His Master's Voice' is prominently displayed—to mention only a few. These enterprising firms, by securing sites for their works alongside the line, have the advantage of direct access to Britain's premier railway, with a considerable saving of haulage between railway and factory. The Great Western Railway Company is now appealing to other firms to follow suit. They are invited to " Settle on the Great Western," and to " Come and see the sites."

We are now travelling at over a mile a minute and approaching Slough, which is the junction for Windsor and Eton. If you will keep a look out on your left after passing Slough Station, you will get a good view of Windsor Castle, the residence of H.M. King George V. When His Majesty is in residence, the Royal Standard flies at the masthead from the tower and at other times the Union Jack is flown. It shews up clearly against the sky-line this morning.

Talking about Eton, you may be interested to know that, when the Great Western Railway was being constructed, a good deal of opposition was met with from different parties who conceived, for reasons which cannot easily be appreciated to-day, a general dislike for railways and a horror of their coming within a reasonable distance. The Eton College Authorities, in righteous apprehension of this new menace to the morals of Eton boys, placed an obligation on the Great Western Railway Company to "maintain a sufficient additional number of persons for the purpose of preventing or restricting all access to the railway by the scholars of Eton College," the appointment, number, control, direction, and dismissal of these persons all being placed in the hands of the College Authorities! These obligations were observed for over forty years, and when the Railway Company secured special powers from Parliament to construct the Windsor Branch, the College Authorities again asserted themselves, with the result that the Company was saddled with the duty of policing the line for the purpose of preventing scholars from getting on to it. All of which is very strange reading for schoolboys to-day.

Between Taplow and Maidenhead Stations we cross Father Thames. Passing Twyford, the junction for Henley (famous for its Royal Regatta), and Sonning Cutting, we get another glimpse of the river, and soon the extensive factory of Messrs. Huntley & Palmer, the biscuit manufacturers, comes into view on your left, for we are

approaching Reading, a progressive town of many historical associations.

Reading enjoys one of the best, if not the best of train services in the country. Hence its popularity as a place of residence for an ever increasing number of business men who travel to and from the City daily.

The Great Western Railway, with its service of frequent non-stop trains in both directions, has brought Reading within forty minutes of London, so that the journey occupies little, if any, more time than in travelling to and from the outer suburbs of the Metropolis.

At Reading we leave the old Great Western Railway main line to the West of England, which passed through Swindon, Bath, and Bristol, for the newer and more direct route through Newbury, Westbury, etc. At Swindon, as you may know, are situated the Locomotive, Carriage and Wagon Works, where the Great Western Railway Company's engines and other rolling stock are built and maintained. I suggest that this would be a convenient opportunity for us to have that promised chat about engines and rolling stock. We will begin with the locomotive.

CHAPTER THE THIRD

LOCOMOTIVES

You will, I expect, be more or less familiar with the history of the evolution of the steam locomotive engine. The glory of its invention was doubtless due in some measure to Watt, Stephenson, and Trevithick. The boy who, when asked who invented the steam engine and replied, " Mr. What's his name ? " was probably thankful that the occasion was an oral examination, and that he was not called upon to " shew his working in the margin."

It is not my intention to trace the various stages of progress of the locomotive from Stephenson's " Rocket," which with a supply of water weighed about four and a half tons, to the modern " hundred tonners," but rather to endeavour to give you a short description of the elementary mechanism and operation of a present-day railway locomotive. Here, I think, some diagrams and photographs will materially assist.

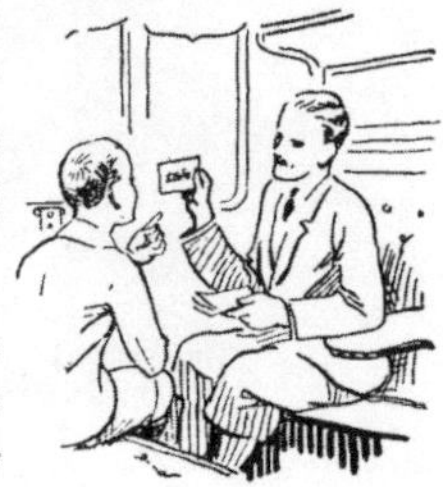

As you will no doubt be aware, steam is generated under pressure in a fire-tube boiler The supply

4 6-0 (TWO CYLINDER) EXPRESS PASSENGER LOCOMOTIVE

By courtesy of the Locomotive Publishing Company.

1—Driving Wheel
2—Leading Coupled Wheel
3—Trailing Coupled Wheel
4—Bogie Wheels
5—Life Guard
6—Cylinder
7—Steam Chest
8—Front Steam Port
9—Back Steam Port
10—Live Steam Space
11—Live Steam Admission Passage
12—Blast Pipe
13, 14—Piston Valves
15—Valve Spindle
16—Reversing Rod
17—Reversing Gear in Cab
18—Reversing Gear Handle
19—Piston
20—Piston Rod
21—Crosshead
22, 23—Slide Bars
24—Connecting Rod
25—Coupling Rod Leading
26—Coupling Rod Trailing
27—Footplate
28—Buffer
29—Screw Coupling
30—Chimney
31—Chimney (internal)
32—Chimney Bell
33—Smoke Box
34—Smoke Box Door
35—Firebox Water Space
36—Fire Door
37—Brick Arch
38—Fire Bars
39—Boiler Barrel
40—Flue Pipes
41—Superheater Flue Pipes
42—Main Steam Pipe
43—Steam Collecting Mouth
44—Regulator Valve
45—Regulator Rod
46—Regulator Handle
47—Steam Pipe to Superheater
48—Superheater Header
49—Safety Valve
50—Live Steam Injector. Steam Water Connection
51—Live Steam Injector. Steam Pipes
52—Injector Steam Valves
53—Whistles
54—Water Gauge
55—Sight Feed Lubricator
56—Cylinder Cock Handle
57—Ashpan
58—Brake Blocks
59—Brake Pull Rods
60—Vacuum Train Pipe
61—Vacuum Train Pipe Coupling
62—Main Vacuum Reservoir
63—Vacuum Ejector
64—Vacuum Brake Pump
65—Sand Pipe
66—Lamp Iron
67—Hand Rail
68—Whistle Handle
69—Fire Hole Door Handle
70—Handle for closing Water Gauge

of steam from the boiler is governed by a regulator valve. After being super-heated (which I will explain a little later on) the steam is distributed by one of the many forms of valve gear into the alternate ends of enclosed cylinders, and its pressure is used to force movable pistons to and fro in the cylinders. Having spent its

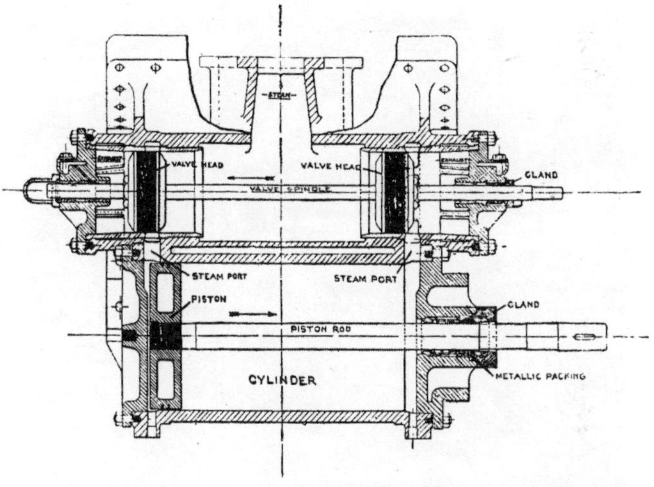

energy, the steam is exhausted through the blast pipe in the smoke-box to the atmosphere via the chimney. The exhausting of the steam through the smoke-box creates a partial vacuum therein, aiding the draught or flow of hot gases through the boiler tubes.

If you will now take a good look at this diagram (which is a section through the piston valve cylinders of an engine) you will see that to each piston is affixed a rod, which passes through a gland in the centre of the back cylinder cover or end. This gland is packed to form a steam-tight joint around the rod, and to the end of the rod outside the cylinder is fixed what is called a " crosshead," which you see in the large diagram and also clearly marked in this photograph. This is virtually a block sliding between two bars. Through

this crosshead is fixed a large pin, and reciprocating motion imparted to the piston, piston rod, and crosshead (all of which move backwards and forwards as one) is converted into the desired rotary motion of the wheels by means of a connecting rod beween the crosshead pin and the crank pin situated in the driving wheel This is clearly demonstrated by the photograph.

The use of inside cylinders renders it necessary to construct the axle of the driving wheels with cranks, as it is impossible to arrange for connecting rods to actuate crank pins attached to the wheels themselves, as is done when the cylinders are placed outside the frames. To counteract the effect of the moving parts (piston and rods, crank, etc.) on the running of the engine, balancing weights are placed on the coupled wheels and secured near the rims. A part of one of these balancing weights can be seen at the bottom of the photograph of the large coupled wheel.

In the modern locomotive, two, three, four, and sometimes five pairs of wheels of the same diameter are connected by coupling rods, mounted upon pins secured to the outside of the wheels and forming the "rigid wheel base."

"Bogie" trucks (those embracing two axles), "pony" trucks (those with one axle), and radial axle-boxes are fitted to enable the locomotive to negotiate curves of small radius.

Compound Locomotives are those in which the steam having passed through one set of cylinders ("high pressure") is again used in relatively larger cylinders ("low pressure") before being finally exhausted and passed into the atmosphere.

There are only three "compound" locomotives working on the Great Western Railway (Numbers 102, 103, and 104). They are of the four-cylinder Atlantic type, the inside (high pressure) cylinders of which drive on to the leading driving axle, and the outside (low pressure) cylinders drive on to the trailing driving axle.

4-6-0 (4-Cylinder) "Star" Class Express Passenger Train

2-8-0 Express Mixed Traffic ("Consolidation") "4700" Class

2-8-0 "Consolidation" "28" Class Express Freight Train

To these cylinders is fitted a device enabling the four cylinders to be worked with high pressure steam, in other words " simple working." This can be employed when necessary, at starting, thus enabling maximum effort to be exerted.

Actual steam distribution into the cylinders of both simple and compound locomotives is the same, and on the large Great Western Railway engines is accomplished by using inside admission piston valves as shewn in the piston-valve diagram.

A piston valve consists of two pistons or " valve-heads " mounted upon a single spindle so as to control the steam passing in and out of the cylinder. If you will look closely at the illustration, I think this will be clear to you.

The regulator valve, opened by the driver, permits steam to pass from the boiler through the superheater into the steam chest (a chamber contained in the cylinder casting) between the valve-heads. In each valve chest are two cylindrical seatings, into which the valve-heads fit and work, and between these seatings live steam enters from the steam chest, and on the outside exhaust steam passes from the cylinders to the blast pipe. In each seating is a port or opening leading to the corresponding end of the engine cylinder. Through these ports steam passes to and from the cylinder, entrance being possible only when the inside edge of the valve-head uncovers a port, and exit only when the outside edge of the valve-head uncovers the same port.

You will see that when steam is admitted to the front end of the cylinder it will force the piston to the back end, and that when steam is admitted to the back end

2-6-0 Express Mixed Traffic "43" Class

4-4-0 "County" Class Passenger Train

2-6-2 "Prairie" Tank Freight Train

of the cylinder and the steam previously admitted to the front end is allowed to escape, the piston will be forced forwards. Thus is reciprocating motion obtained.

When the engine is started steam is admitted for three quarters of the whole period of piston travel, but after starting the driver restricts the travel of the valves by "notching up" his reversing-gear lever and thereby causes the valves to close the port earlier. After this operation—known as the "cut-off"—has taken place the steam in the cylinder works expansively.

The driver varies this period of steam admission, or position of "cut-off," according to the speed. At high speeds engines are worked at "early cut-off," and at slow speeds "late cut-off."

The valve gears principally used on the locomotives of the Great Western Railway are Stephenson's link motion, Walschaërt's valve gear, and gears of its own design.

Stephenson's link motion for one cylinder briefly consists of the following:

Two eccentrics keyed to the axle of the driving wheels act as cranks, the "throw" of which is about half the maximum travel of the valve. One of these eccentrics controls the forward, and the other the backward motion of the valve. Working around these eccentrics are "straps" to which rods are attached. These rods are forked at their forward extremities and between them, in the forks, is fitted a curved link, termed the "expansion link," the "forward" eccentric rod being attached to the top of the link and the "backward" rod to the bottom.

The link is supported by others, known as "suspension links," which are attached to a reversing shaft above, an arm of which communicates by means of a rod with a reversing handle in the cab of the locomotive.

The expansion link can be either raised or lowered, effecting the reversing of the engine. It also governs the travel given to the valve, and thus varies the periods of admission and expansion of steam in the cylinders.

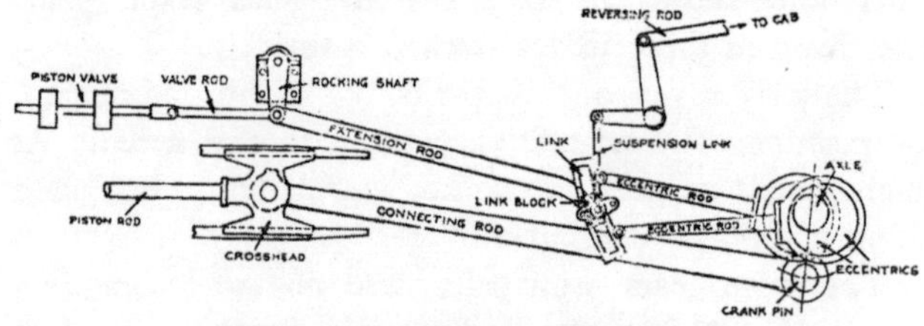

Diagram of Stephenson Link Motion

The extension rod which connects the valve to the link is forked at both ends, the rear enclosing both the link and also the block working in the slot of the link, and the front end attached to a "rocking shaft." To the rocking shaft, but outside the frames, is also connected the valve spindle through an intermediate rod.

When the link is lowered as far as possible, the valve spindle is influenced by the "forward" eccentric, and in this position, known as "full fore gear," and when steam is admitted to the cylinders, the engine moves forward.

Contrariwise, when the link is raised, the effect of the "backward" eccentric is felt and the engine moves backward. This is known as "full back gear."

" Mid gear " is when the link is positioned centrally so that the eccentrics are counteracting the action of one another.

If this is getting just a little technical, I am afraid it is to some extent unavoidable. You can, however, take courage. The worst is past. There are no horrible equations to worry you, and I can assure you that " *x* " will remain very much an unknown quantity as far as we are concerned to-day.

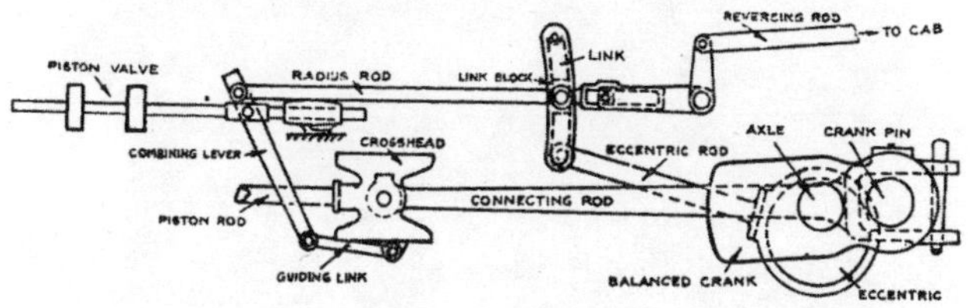

Diagram of Walschaërt Valve Gear

Walschaërt's valve gear is fitted to the compound locomotives already mentioned, engines of 4000 class, and to Great Western Railway rail motors. It requires only one eccentric, and is usually fitted outside the frames. On the Great Western Railway four-cylinder engines of the 4000 class, however, two sets actuate all cylinders, the outside cylinders being worked by means of rocking levers from the inside motion.

This mechanism is a little intricate and, perhaps, somewhat difficult to describe briefly without technicalities, but if you will closely study the diagram, I think you will be able to follow it.

Lubrication of the cylinders and regulator valve is

effected by feeding oil from a displacement lubricator into the steam in the regulator box and in the steam pipes, between the superheater and steam chest, by which it is carried in the form of spray to the surfaces requiring lubrication. This lubricator is controlled by

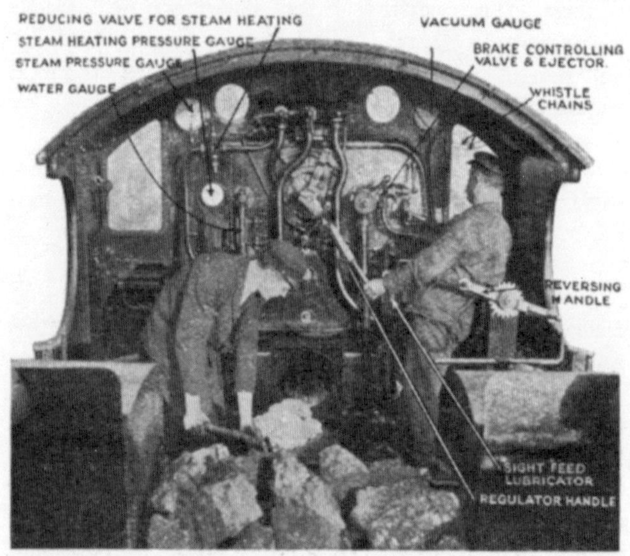

the regulator handle, so that lubrication is supplied only when the engine is in motion.

All other lubrication is effected by percolation of oil through short lengths of absorbent "trimmings" from receptacles or cups to the bearing surfaces; the cups being filled by the driver before the trip or during stops.

Superheating is very simple—it is the heating of steam,

after it has ceased to be in contact with water, above its generation temperature.

Three results are achieved by superheating, which greatly improve the efficiency of the locomotive to which the superheater is fitted, viz. :

1. Water held in suspension is converted into steam.
2. Provision is made against condensation of steam by the reserve of heat.
3. The volume of steam is greatly increased.

Of the many superheaters in use, the " Swindon " superheater, designed and used by the Great Western Railway Company on its locomotives, is the most simple, and ranks amongst the most efficient.

Now, if you have listened attentively to the descriptions I have endeavoured to give you, and carefully studied each of the diagrams and photographs meanwhile, you should, I think, have acquired an elementary knowledge of some of the main principles of locomotive mechanism and operation.

We have referred once or twice to types and classes of locomotives and also to wheel arrangement classifications. Some years ago it was the custom to refer to particular types of engines as " four wheels coupled," " six wheels coupled," or " singles," etc. This classification was useful, but need existed for some means of identification which would be simple, easily understood, and more concisely expressed, and a new system of classification was gradually adopted. It is based upon the representation by numerals of the number and arrangement of the wheels of a locomotive beginning at the

THE "SWINDON" SUPERHEATER

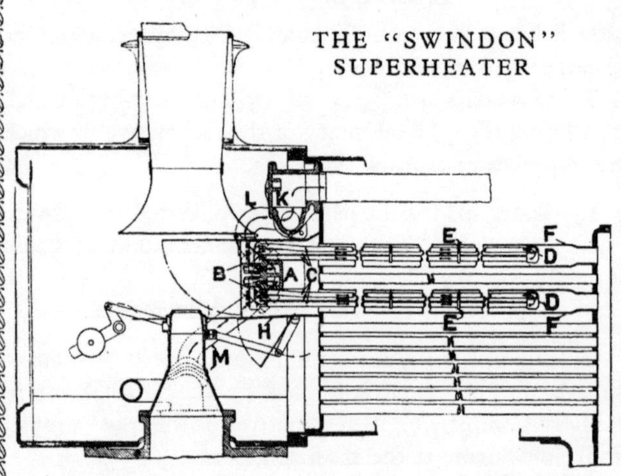

The Superheater consists of a main header, "A," stretching across the smoke-box; a number of U-shaped junction headers, "B," extending like fingers at the top and bottom of the main header, to which they are bolted, and a series of superheater tubes, "C," expanded into the junction header and terminating in bends, "D." These tubes are stiffened by perforated plate supports, "E," through which they are passed, and project into two rows of large flues, "F," in the boiler. The supports have the additional advantage of disturbing and "churning up" the heated gases as they pass through the flues. The whole of the smoke-box portion is enclosed by plates. The front is hinged to provide access to the superheater, and the bottom forms a damper, "H," the normal position of which is closed, but it is automatically opened by a small steam cylinder actuated by the regulator handle on the footplate. After its production in the boiler, steam passes through the regulator, "K," and the steampipe, "L," to the top chamber of the main header, "A," thence to one finger of the junction headers, "B," through the small superheater tubes, "C," to the other finger, thence to the bottom chamber of the header and through the steampipes, "M," to the cylinders

front. Thus 4–6–0 denotes a ten-wheeled engine, the use of the cipher shewing that there are no trailing wheels, i.e., carrying wheels behind the drivers. This little diagram of another type, viz., 4–4–2, will, I think, make my meaning clear:

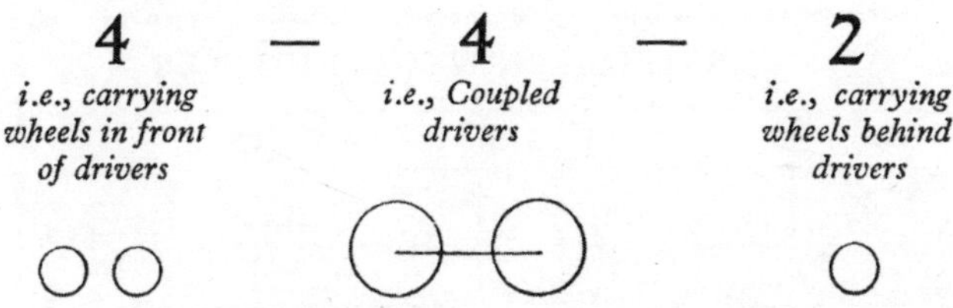

The wheels on one side only of the engine are indicated by the circles, but the wheels of a locomotive, like the legs of a horse, always consist of "an equal number on each side."

To distinguish between "Tender" and "Tank" engines the letter T in the latter case is placed under the numerals thus: $\frac{4\text{–}4\text{–}2}{\text{T}}$. This classification here diagrammatically illustrated answers all purposes.

The terms often used to designate certain types of engines, such as "Consolidation" (2–8–0), "Prairie" (2–6–0), "Atlantic" (4–4–2), "Pacific" (4–6–2), are American in origin.

You will have observed that many of the Great Western Railway passenger train engines bear names as well as numbers. These names also run in classes, such as the "County" Class (4–4–0)—"County of Middlesex," "County of Bedford," etc.; "Star" Class (4–6–0)—

"North Star," "Evening Star," etc.; "Saint" Class (4–6–0)—"Saint David," "Saint George," etc.

There is also a numerical classification, e.g., the "4000" class—four-cylinder 4–6–0 type. These photographs of a few typical Great Western Railway engines will assist

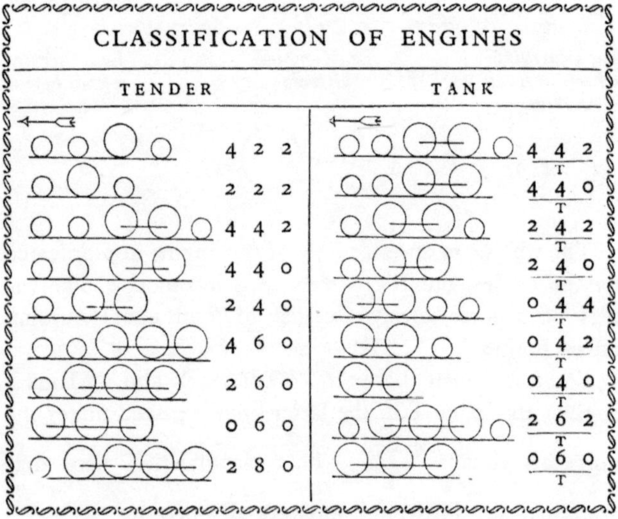

CLASSIFICATION OF ENGINES

TENDER	TANK
4 2 2	4 4 2 T
2 2 2	4 4 0 T
4 4 2	2 4 2 T
4 4 0	2 4 0 T
2 4 0	0 4 4 T
4 6 0	0 4 2 T
2 6 0	0 4 0 T
0 6 0	2 6 2 T
2 8 0	0 6 0 T

you in following these various classifications, but for those who would know more upon the subject, a booklet is available.*

Locomotives may be broadly classified into passenger train, freight train, and shunting engines, and each of these classes further divided according to the nature of

* *"Great Western Railway Engines: Names, Numbers, Types, and Classes"* (1s.). *Published by "Great Western Railway Magazine," Paddington Station, London, W. 2.*

4—6—2 (FOUR-CYLINDER) "PACIFIC"

Cylinders—Four—Dia., 15″; Stroke, 26″. *Boiler*—Barrel, 23′ 0″; Dia. outside, 5′ 6″ and 6′ 0″.
Heating Surface, including Superheater—3,154·00 Sq. Ft.
Wheels—Bogie, 3′ 2″; Driving and Intermediate, 6′ 8½″; Trailing, 3′ 8″.
Water Capacity of Tender—3,500 Gallons. *Working Pressure*—225 Lbs. *Tractive Effort*—27,800 Lbs.

the work the engines are required to perform, the loads they have to haul, the speeds at which they are required to run, and the gradients of the lines on which they are employed.

The power of a locomotive depends upon boiler capacity, tractive force and drawbar pull (which may be shortly defined as the force exerted at the driving wheels and capacity to haul loads), and adhesive force, which depends upon the weight on the driving wheels and the friction between wheels and rails. Coupling wheels together increases adhesion, and this is why engines with a number of wheels coupled, such as the 2–8–0 class, are used for heavy freight trains, as nearly the whole of the weight of the engine is available for adhesion and the smaller wheels give tractive force. Such an engine would not, of course, be suitable for fast passenger trains.

The four-cylinder 4000 class and the two-cylinder 2900 class (both 4–6–0) are examples of locomotives designed for hauling heavy passenger trains at high speed. Both these engines are of large boiler capacity and have six coupled driving wheels of 6 ft. 8½ ins. diameter.

"The Great Bear," the largest Great Western Railway passenger train engine, was the originator of the 4–6–2 "Pacific" Class in this country, where for some ten years it was the only representative of its class. The first locomotive run on the Great Western Railway was the "Vulcan," built by the Vulcan Foundry Company, which you will see contrasts strikingly with "The Great Bear."

Towards the end of August this year the Great Western Railway turned out from its Swindon Works the first of a batch of ten new engines to be known as the "Castle" Class. The "Caerphilly Castle," No. 4073, a four-cylinder locomotive (4–6–0), embraces several new and important departures from the design of previous engines of the same type.

Larger cylinders have been fitted, and to supply them with steam a new boiler has been designed. While retaining the special features of the G.W.R. standard boilers, some of the dimensions have been increased. The inside cylinders are supplied with steam through passages in the saddle supporting the smoke-box, the steam pipes for the outside cylinders being brought through the side of the smoke-box and connected direct to the steam chests.

The larger cylinders bring the tractive effort up to 31,625 lbs. at 85 per cent. boiler pressure, compared with 27,800 of the present four-cylinder class, thus making the new engine the most powerful express passenger locomotive in the British Isles.

The provision of a longer cab has been possible owing to the increased length of the frame. This, coupled with the fact that no fittings project into the cab beyond the regulator handle, gives greatly increased space for the driver and fireman. The roof has also been considerably extended and the cab sides fitted with large windows, a further innovation being the provision of tip-up seats for the driver and fireman.

The general finish of the engine is admirable. The chimney has a copper top, and there is a brass safety-valve cover. The cab and splasher beadings are in brass, and the hand rails are polished.

"*CAERPHILLY CASTLE*". THE NEW GREAT WESTERN 4-6-0 ENGINE

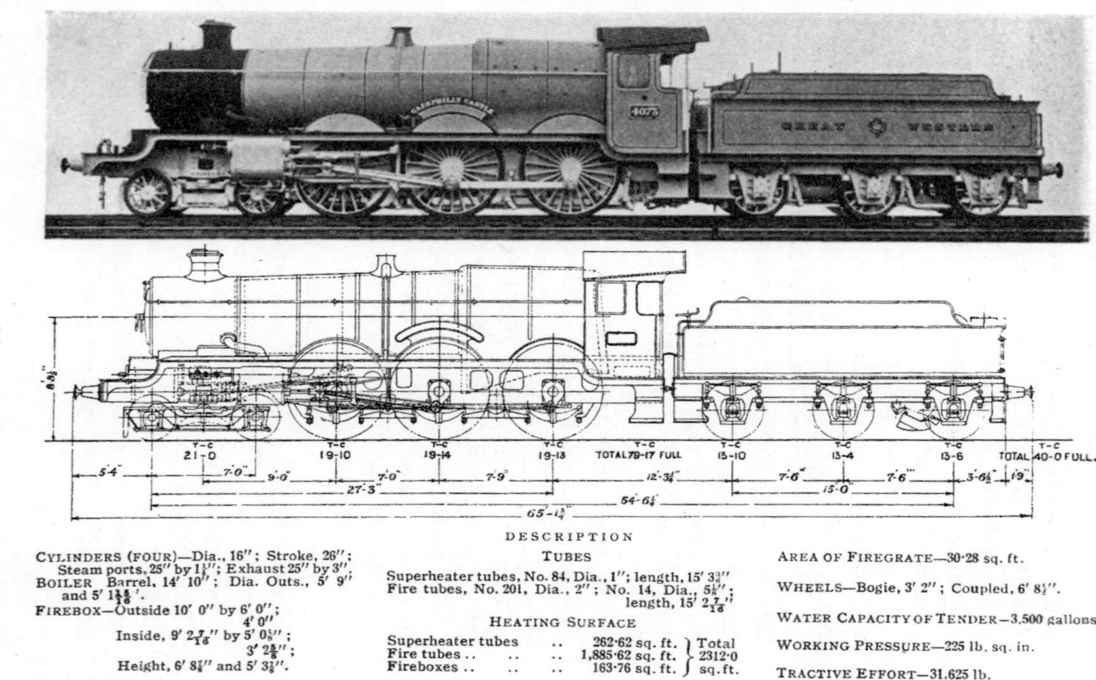

DESCRIPTION

CYLINDERS (FOUR)—Dia., 16″; Stroke, 26″; Steam ports, 25″ by $1\frac{1}{4}$″; Exhaust 25″ by 3″.

BOILER Barrel, 14′ 10″; Dia. Outs., 5′ 9″ and 5′ $1\frac{15}{16}$″.

FIREBOX—Outside 10′ 0″ by 6′ 0″; 4′ 0″
Inside, 9′ $2\frac{7}{16}$″ by 5′ $0\frac{1}{8}$″; 3′ $2\frac{5}{8}$″;
Height, 6′ $8\frac{7}{8}$″ and 5′ $3\frac{3}{8}$″.

TUBES

Superheater tubes, No. 84, Dia., 1″; length, 15′ $3\frac{3}{8}$″
Fire tubes, No. 201, Dia., 2″; No. 14, Dia., $5\frac{1}{8}$″; length, 15′ $2\frac{7}{16}$″

HEATING SURFACE

Superheater tubes ..	262·62 sq. ft.	Total 2312·0 sq. ft.
Fire tubes	1,885·62 sq. ft.	
Fireboxes	163·76 sq. ft.	

AREA OF FIREGRATE—30·28 sq. ft.

WHEELS—Bogie, 3′ 2″; Coupled, 6′ $8\frac{1}{2}$″.

WATER CAPACITY OF TENDER—3,500 gallons

WORKING PRESSURE—225 lb. sq. in.

TRACTIVE EFFORT—31,625 lb.

This is the first engine to be turned out of the Swindon Works with lined-out panels, boiler bands, etc., since the war. You may be interested to know that all engines of the 2900 and 4000 classes will in future be similarly finished as they pass through the Swindon shops.

Interior of one of the Erecting Shops, Swindon Works

The Swindon Works (established in 1842), where the Company's locomotives and rolling stock are built and maintained, are amongst the most extensive in the world, occupying an area of 310 acres, of which 65 are roofed.

The number of men employed at Swindon Works has increased from 4,500 in 1876 to 13,500 at the present time.

CHAPTER THE FOURTH

WATER AND FUEL

It is thirsty work to run two hundred and twenty-six miles without a stop, and on the journey to Plymouth our engine will need refreshing to the extent of some thirty-four tons of water. The water storage capacity of the tender is about three thousand five hundred gallons, and the supply is replenished from water-troughs laid between the rails as the train is running at high speed. It is this means of taking water *en route* which enables engines of relatively small water storage capacity to make long non-stop runs.

A hinged scoop, not unlike a shovel in shape, is fitted under the engine tender, and controlled from the foot-plate. Lowered by the fireman when running over the water-troughs, the scoop cuts off, as it were, the top layer of the water, which the speed of the train forces up an internal vertical pipe leading from the scoop to the tank. The end of this pipe is carried above the maximum water-level, and just above it is fitted an inverted dish to deflect the water down into the tank wherein it is trapped. Air displaced escapes through air vents, and a water-indicator records the amount of water in the tank, the fireman raising the scoop accordingly. Anything from two thousand to three thousand gallons of water is by this means picked up in about fifteen to twenty seconds. The speed of the train when thus picking up water is from fifty to sixty miles an hour.

To permit of lowering the scoop from the footplate just previous to reaching the troughs and raising it after passing, the rails at each end of the troughs are laid for a distance of 180 feet on a down gradient of 1 in 360, in each case towards the centre of the troughs. The tender passing over the down gradient causes the scoop, which though lowered by the fireman is yet above the troughs, to be further lowered 2 inches below the water-level. If the scoop is not previously raised by the fireman, the up gradient at the far end of the troughs will lift it clear.

The longest water-troughs on the Great Western Railway are 1,838 feet in length over-all, and are made in 10-foot lengths of galvanised steel plate approximately 6 inches deep and 18 inches wide, the top edges being turned in slightly, forming lips to avoid unnecessary waste. The troughs are laid on light steel brackets bolted to the sleepers between the rails, and at the ends the bottom inclines gradually with the gradient to the top, thereby trapping the water.

The principle of the apparatus used for replenishing the troughs and controlling the water-level is that of the ball valve of the household cistern. The buoyant body in this case is a large float, which, rising and falling with the fluctuating water-level in the troughs, sensitively controls, through a long arm, an equilibrium valve of sufficient dimensions to permit quick replacement of water picked up.

This apparatus is housed in a small building alongside the line, and is arranged with the float tank on the level of the troughs, so that when water is taken from the troughs the level in the float tank drops. The consequent lowering of the float opens the equilibrium valve, permitting a rush of water from a large overhead tank into the supply pipe, which divides and runs 333 feet towards each end of the troughs before delivering into them. This delivery at two points causes a flow in four separate streams, quickly distributing the supply and reducing the height of the wave.

From what has been said you will appreciate that water-troughs can only be provided (except at very considerable expense) where the circumstances are favourable; and where this equipment is installed, three main conditions are desirable:

1. The track must be level.
2. A plentiful supply of water must be obtainable with a minimum of pumping and purification or softening before being suitable for use in boilers.
3. The site must be sufficiently distant from signals to permit trains, which may be checked or stopped at the next signal, to travel over the troughs fast enough to pick up water efficiently.

On the run from Paddington to Plymouth we pick up water at Aldermaston; near Westbury; at Creech, and between Starcross and Exminster.

WATER AND FUEL

Just a word about fuel before we leave the subject of the locomotive. For the trip from London to Plymouth our four-cylinder express engine will consume (on the average) some thirty-eight pounds of coal per mile run, or a total quantity of nearly four tons. All this coal has, of course, to be handled by the fireman and placed scientifically on the fire if the best results are to be obtained. He carries out his work whilst the train is running at high speed, so you can appreciate that, whilst we are sitting here in ease and comfort, the fireman on the footplate is being kept pretty busy.

CHAPTER THE FIFTH

CARRIAGES

THE coach in which we are travelling so comfortably and speedily this morning is one of the Great Western Railway standard seventy-foot corridor coaches, the longest coaching stock in use in the United Kingdom ; the actual length over the buffers is 73 feet 6 inches.

These vehicles, like practically all the Great Western locomotive, coaching, and wagon stock, are built at the Company's works at Swindon. They are self-lit by electricity, steam-heated, and fitted throughout with the vacuum brake and amply provided with lavatory accommodation. In all principal long-distance trains restaurant cars are provided.

The policy of the Great Western Railway is a progressive one in the matter of rolling-stock production as in other directions, and there are now coming into traffic and on the stocks at Swindon entirely new trains, including dining-cars, fitted with automatic couplings and a number of new devices. You will, I know, like to have some particulars of these new vehicles, which represent the very last word in railway passenger-carriage construction.

The outstanding constructional feature of the new trains is that the coaches are fitted at each end with

Laycock " Buckeye " automatic couplers and gangways. The effect of this provision is that the pressure normally distributed between the buffers is transferred to four powerful springs placed one in each corner of the face-plates of the corridor gangways, the result being that with the even distribution of pressure over the entire end of the coach, the train becomes somewhat like a flexible tube. In running, oscillation is reduced to a

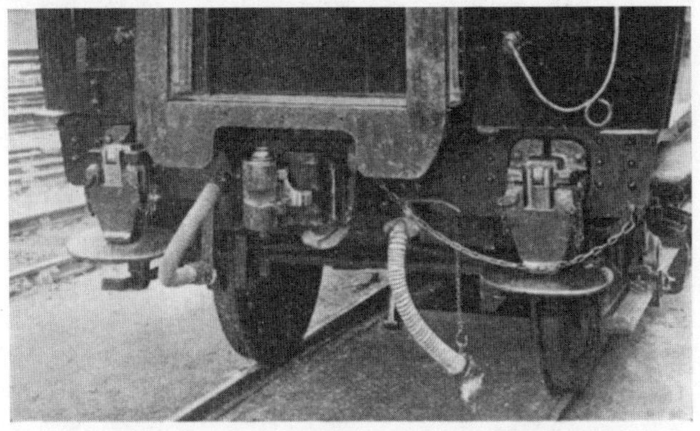

minimum, and there is much greater flexibility when taking curves. Another important factor in the introduction of automatic couplers is the additional safety they afford to the staff.

Specially designed " drop-down " side buffers and gangway adapters are provided, where " Buckeye " couplers are used, to enable the automatic coupler-fitted coaches to be connected to coaches with the existing standard gangways and screw couplings. The special buffers are dropped down, with their heads

1—Royal Saloon 2—Third-class Corridor Coach (70 ft.) 3—Ocean Mails Van (70 ft.)

hanging towards the track, whilst the automatic coupler is in use, and in the reverse case, i.e. when ordinary screw couplings are required to be utilised, the automatic coupler head is dropped in a similar manner, exposing a drawbar hook, to which the screw coupling is attached, the buffers then being raised and secured in the horizontal position.

Four-wheel metal-frame bogies are used under the

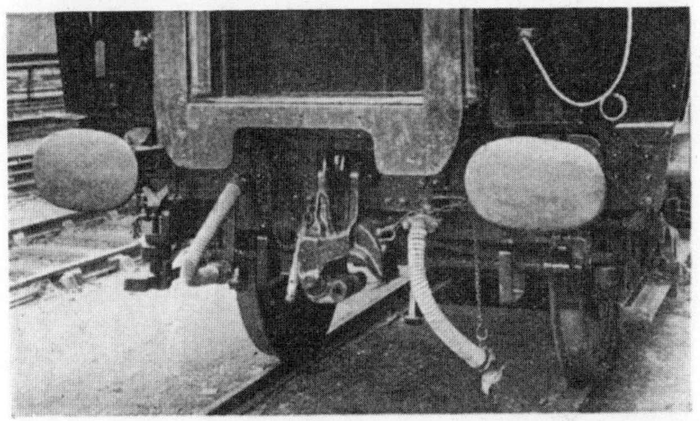

coaches. The special feature in the design of this bogie is the bolster suspension arrangement. Vertical suspension bolts, two at each corner of the bogie bolster, are arranged so that the points of suspension are as far as possible from the centre of the bogie, to ensure steadiness in riding. Two spherical washers are provided on each suspension bolt, one under the bolster spring and one over the suspension bracket on the bogie frame, to allow free movement of the bolster. The suspension bolts are arranged vertically to overcome the see-saw move-

1—30-ton Timber Truck (50 ft.). 2—14-ton Open Goods Wagon
3—20-ton Hopper Ballast Wagon. 4—Cattle Wagon.

ment which obtains in bolster bogies with inclined bolster sling joints.

Each composite coach has four first-class and five third-class compartments, seating twenty-four first- and forty third-class passengers, a door in the corridor dividing first and third.

Each first-class compartment is upholstered in brown cloth, with brown and gold lace. The floor is covered with linoleum; a brown rug, with border and Great Western Railway monogram in black, extends from door to door. Antimacassars are provided for the tops of seat backs, and a double-looped arm sling is secured to each door pillar.

The third-class coaches have ten compartments, with seating accommodation for eighty passengers. The upholstery is black and red rep, red being predominant, and the floor is covered with linoleum. A smaller arm rest than that previously used is fixed below each window; this gives increased seating space.

Lavatory accommodation is provided at both ends of each of these coaches.

The ceilings in all compartments are of birchwood veneer, enamelled white to assist the lighting. Three electric lights are arranged in the ceiling in a straight row between the doors in each third-class compartment, and in each first-class compartment there are five, one in the centre of the ceiling and one over each corner seat. These latter are controlled by a switch in each corner, which can be operated by the passenger near it. A switch is provided for dimming the centre light in each compartment.

1—Milk Van (50 ft.)
2—Open Scenery Truck (50 ft.)
3—Horse Box
4—Refrigerator Meat Van

To obtain steady riding, the dining-cars of these new trains have been designed with kitchen and pantry in the centre, with the first-class saloon at one end, and the third-class at the other end of the vehicles. These cars will accommodate eighteen first-class and thirty-two

King's Saloon, Royal Train

third-class diners. The seats in both saloon compartments are of the " tip-up " type, upholstered in brown leather.

On the floors carpet is laid upon linoleum. The interior finishing in the first-class saloons is in rich dark polished walnut, with sycamore panels, and in the third-class saloons in polished mahogany. Electric fans and bells are provided, and the cars are well lighted throughout by electricity. Special attention has been given to ventilation; in addition to the top portion of each side light being hinged to open, the air extractors on the roof have been modified. Instead of passing direct through the outside roof and ceiling into the compartment, they pass through the outside roof into the space between the roof and ceiling, extracting the air from positions immediately above the dining-tables, the projecting lips for manipulating the extractors being within easy reach of the passengers. This arrangement prevents ashes or dust passing into the saloons.

We have not, I fear, time to consider the many types of rolling stock in use, but these photographs represent a small selection and will give you some idea of the variety of vehicles which a railway company has to provide for the conveyance of its miscellaneous traffics, which include everything from magic lanterns to molasses, and door-knobs to dromedaries.

CHAPTER THE SIXTH

TRAIN LIGHTING AND HEATING

IF there is one subject which appears rather more mystifying than another in connection with modern railway practice, it is probably the electric lighting of the coaches. On electrified railways the lighting is a comparatively simple matter, as the electricity is available for driving and heating the train, and it can be utilised with equal convenience for illumination. The " shoes " or collectors in contact with the conductor rail or overhead wires collect the electricity and the cables connected with the shoes distribute the current throughout the train for any or all the purposes required. With few exceptions, however, the railway lines in this country connecting cities and towns are constructed for steam traction, and other means have to be found to provide electricity for lighting the trains.

In the early days, trains were lighted by means of oil lamps. Then came the flat flame gas-burner using compressed oil gas. This was followed by the inverted incandescent gas-burners, an excellent illuminant, but with some disadvantages. As you see, the modern coaches in which we are now travelling are all fitted for electric lighting, and for many years past all new carriages constructed by the Great Western Railway have been electrically lighted. You will probably be curious to know how this is done.

Perhaps you have paid a visit to an electric generating station and seen the powerful steam engines and dynamos employed for producing electricity for use in our homes,

Dynamo under Coach

workshops, etc. If you have been so fortunate, you will know something of the means employed for generating electricity and for controlling it in order that it may be suitable for the many purposes for which it is used.

Situated under each electrically lighted railway coach is what is, in effect, a small electric generating station, but in place of the men employed in a large electric power station we have automatic control of the supply of electricity.

Our small generating station is a veritable "multum in parvo" consisting of a dynamo, battery, and automatic controller. The chief difference between it and the generating stations with which you are more familiar, apart from size and capacity, is that with the under-coach generating station the dynamo is driven from the coach wheels, which are running at continually varying speeds and sometimes not moving at all. You will appreciate that the lighting of the coaches has to remain constant whether the train is running fast, slow, or even standing at a station or elsewhere. The pressure at which the dynamo delivers electricity to the coach will, within certain limits, depend on the speed of the train, and, as the speed is continually varying, means have to be found for maintaining a steady electrical pressure essential to the lamps, etc., and a varying electrical pressure essential to charging the battery.

Regulator

The lamp pressure on the Great Western Railway is twenty-two volts, and any pressure below or above that will produce a correspondingly dull or brilliant light. The latter condition would lead to early destruction of the lamps. The battery requires a pressure up to thirty-three volts to charge it fully, and the automatic control must be capable of providing for this varying pressure for the battery, the steady pressure for the lamps, and the varying speed of the dynamo. The regulator, which is in effect an automatic "switchboard attendant," is responsible for doing all these things.

Battery under Coach

The dynamo is driven by means of a belt from a pulley fixed to one of the bogie axles of the coach, and it must work equally well whichever way the coach is travelling. It is suspended in such a manner that it may be free to swivel and relieve or maintain the belt tension due to the pivoting of the bogie when the coach is running on curves. Below speeds of about twenty-five miles per hour the dynamo is unable to generate electricity at a pressure sufficient for the lamps or battery, but at about that speed the automatic switch comes into play, connects the dynamo to the lamps and battery, and from then onwards it is able to generate electricity in such quantities and at all speeds between twenty-five miles per hour and ninety miles per hour as to meet the needs of the lamps fitted in the coaches and also for charging the battery.

While the train is running at or above twenty-five miles per hour the dynamo generates electricity at a proper pressure for the lamps and battery, but as the train slows down the pressure drops, and the automatic switch disconnects the dynamo from the lamps and battery. Until the train is again running at twenty-five miles per hour the battery alone takes up the work of supplying electric current for lighting the coach. The battery may be regarded as a tank into which the dynamo pumps all the electric current—familiarly known as the "juice"—generated and not being used by the lamps. From this battery the lamps can draw a supply of current when the train is stationary or running at a speed less than twenty-five miles per hour.

Automatic Switch

To charge the battery fully, the pressure across the terminals of the dynamo must be gradually raised to thirty-three volts. This pressure is much higher than the lamps can stand, and our friend the "switch board attendant" or regulator, while taking care that the battery gets all the pressure it wants, sees that the extra pressure which would be injurious to the lamps is cut off and the charging of the battery automatically stopped when it has been loaded to its capacity.

A distant switch is provided and enables the lights for the whole train to be turned on or off from any coach in the train or for the lights for a single coach to be switched on or off from the coach itself.

From what has been said, I think you will agree that our small generating station is a wonderful piece of mechanism. We have a dynamo capable of working automatically equally well whichever way it is revolving, and of standing speeds up to ninety miles per hour, which means over two thousand revolutions per minute for the dynamo shaft. It is liable to deluges from the locomotive when picking up water at speed from the troughs, and is sometimes away from a repair shop for many weeks at a stretch. As you will realise, in all these respects it is at a disadvantage compared with the large power stations from which we draw our domestic supplies. Despite all this, it stands up to its work remarkably well and, considering all things, failures of the delicate and largely automatic mechanism are few and far between.

During the winter months provision has to be made for heating the trains, and this is accomplished by passing live steam from the boiler of the engine at a reduced pressure through a pipe system running the length of

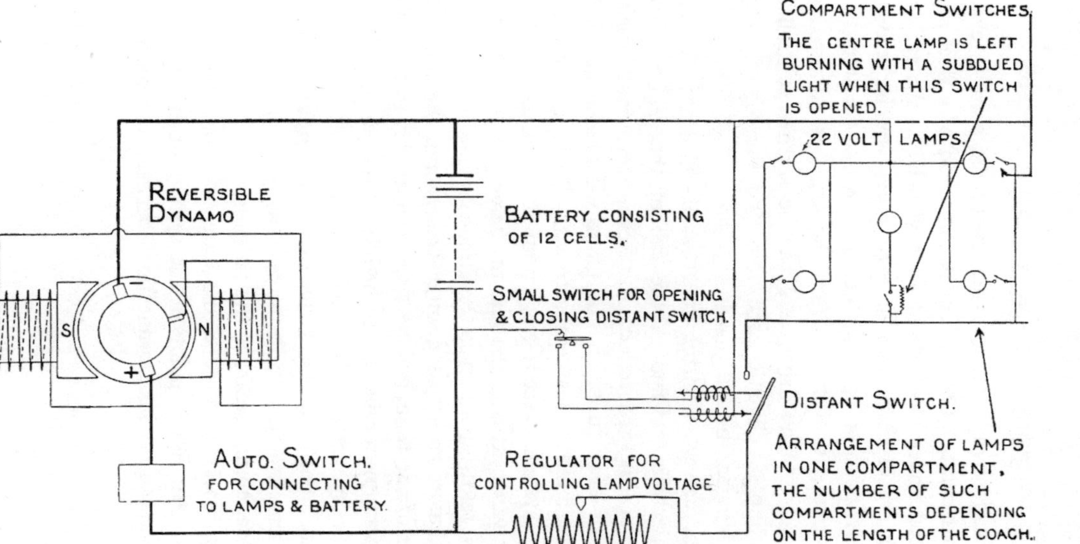

Diagram of Electric Lighting of Passenger Coach

the train to radiators situated under the seats in every compartment. This system is composed of a steel pipe situated under the floor of each vehicle, at the ends of which are fitted flexible hose couplings similar, though smaller, to those used on the vacuum brake system.

The supply of steam from the boiler is admitted to the train by the driver and can be further controlled, according to climatic conditions and the requirements of passengers, by the guard.

The driver's control consists of a steam-reducing valve, which is fitted in the cab of the engine. The action of this valve reduces the steam pressure and maintains an even supply. The guard's control consists of a valve fitted in his compartment. When the pressure in the system exceeds sixty pounds per square inch, a check valve fitted to the rear of the engine automatically opens, releasing steam to the atmosphere.

Radiators are situated under the seats in the compartments of the train, and heating is controlled in the compartment by means of the handle which you see under the luggage rack. This handle, when placed in the "Cold" position, closes the valve and prevents steam from entering the radiator, and when in the "Hot" position, admits steam to the radiator.

Drip cocks to disperse the water of condensation are fitted at the lowest points of the system—namely, on the couplings of the hose connections between the coaches.

TO STOP THE TRAIN IN CASE
OF EMERGENCY
PULL DOWN THE CHAIN
PENALTY FOR IMPROPER USE £5

CHAPTER THE SEVENTH

THE VACUUM BRAKE

YOU have probably read this notice, which is in every Great Western Railway passenger compartment, many times, and wondered just how the action of pulling the chain brings the train to a stop. You are not the first boy who has been curious on this point. In order to test their ideas of money values, the scholars in a certain school were asked to write an essay, the subject being "How I would spend £5," and one boy with some originality expressed the considered opinion that he would take a journey in a fast train, pull the emergency chain, and see what happened! I will endeavour to explain just what does happen, but we won't pull the chain and incur the £5 penalty, if you *don't* mind.

The effect of pulling the emergency chain is partially to apply the vacuum brake, which is continuous throughout the whole of the train. As a certain amount of vacuum is lost, it would be at once indicated on the vacuum gauges on the engine and in the guard's van. Further, a pair of small discs would be exhibited (one on each side) at the end of the coach in which the chain was pulled, and as the emergency chain remains slack after being pulled, the guard would have no trouble in ascertaining the particular compartment concerned.

The engine-driver, on feeling a partial application of the vacuum brake and seeing the indication on the vacuum gauge fixed on the engine, would at once infer that the emergency chain had been pulled and bring his train to a stand as soon as possible.

This brings us to consideration of the vacuum brake, of which the passenger communication is one adaptation.

Among the many libels on schoolboys of the age is the alleged perpetration of a "howler" in which one of your fraternity defined a vacuum as "the place in which the Pope lives." This is, of course, first cousin to the classic definition of the equator as "a menagerie lion running round the world" and probably equally authentic. A more accurate and scientific definition of a vacuum, however, is "a space absolutely devoid of any matter capable of exerting pressure." You probably know that such a thing as a perfect vacuum is not obtainable, and we have to be content with a partial vacuum, which, to all intents and purposes, is what is meant when the word vacuum is used.

Briefly, the railway automatic vacuum brake consists of an air-exhausting device on the engine and a continuous vacuum pipe throughout the train from which, under ordinary conditions, air is exhausted; and a brake cylinder and vacuum reservoir combined under each coach of a train. The coaches are connected by means of flexible hosepipes for braking purposes.

If you will have a look at this diagram, which illustrates the position of the cylinder and vacuum chamber

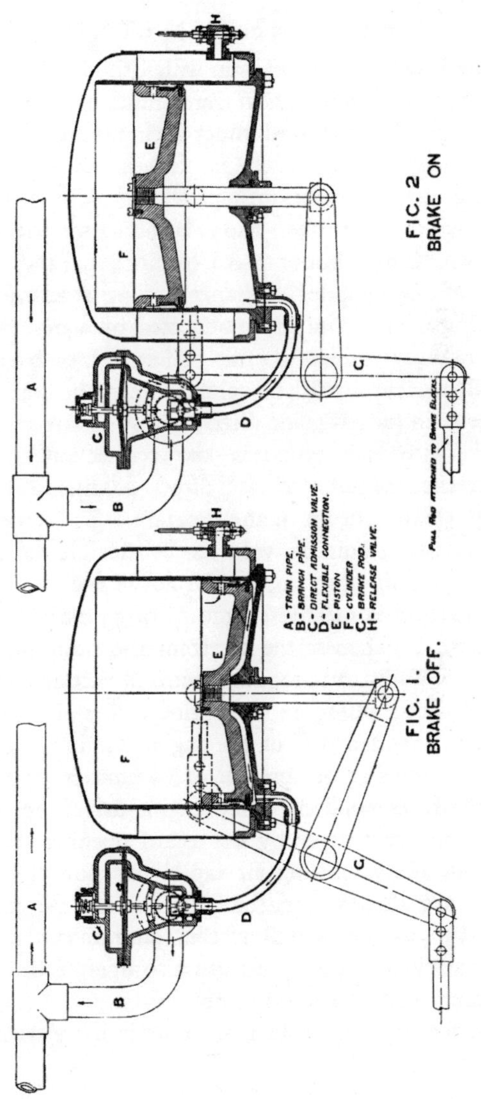

Vacuum Brake Apparatus

when the brake is on or off, you will, I think, get a pretty clear appreciation of just how the vacuum brake operates.

Brake cylinders are fixed under each passenger vehicle, and on long coaches such as that in which we are travelling, two cylinders are provided. The piston is surrounded by a rubber flap which allows the air to be drawn from, but not to return to, the upper portion of the cylinder and surrounding reservoir. As you will see, the cylinder is connected by a branch pipe to the train pipe which extends underneath each vehicle. On small vehicles, with one cylinder only, the connection with the train pipe is made direct, whilst on large vehicles like this with two cylinders the connection is made through the medium of a "direct admission" valve which is clearly shewn in the diagram. The train pipe connects with adjoining vehicles by flexible hosepipes which rest on air-tight stops when not in use.

The vacuum is created by means of an ejector on the engine which exhausts the air from the train pipe and cylinders. Whilst running, the required vacuum is maintained by an air pump on the engine and, as I have said, gauges are provided both on the engine and in the guard's van, which register the amount of vacuum created.

The brake is applied by the engine-driver opening a valve on the engine, or by the guard opening the cock in his van and admitting air rapidly or slowly, at will. As you have already seen, the brake can also be partially applied by passengers pulling the communication chain in emergency, and the guard can also operate the brake by opening the brake setter in his van.

When the brake is applied, air flows into the train pipe

and raises the diaphragm of the "direct admission" valve. The air from the atmosphere is thus admitted through the top valve and flows to the lower portion of the cylinder in sufficient quantity to reduce the vacuum to the same amount as in the train pipe. The pressure of the air in the cylinder raises the piston, and by this means actuates the brake rods by which the brake blocks are applied to the wheels of the coach. The brake is released either by the engine-driver recreating the vacuum or by the release valves of the cylinder being opened and so admitting air to the upper side of the piston and equalising the pressure.

The main features of the vacuum brake may be briefly summarised as follows:

1. It is continuous in its action.
2. It can be applied over the whole length of the train and engine at the same time.
3. It can be worked upon trains of any length without difficulty.
4. It can be applied either by the engine-driver, the guard, or a passenger.
5. It is automatically operated on both portions in the event of a train parting.

The last point needs no explanation, as you will readily understand that in the event of any severance of the flexible hosepipes the vacuum would be destroyed and the brake applied.

A number of vehicles on the Great Western Railway are dually fitted, i.e. with both the vacuum and the Westinghouse brake equipment, so that they may travel on railways using the latter type of brake, thus obviating the necessity for passengers to change coaches at junctions with other railways.

In addition to the automatic vacuum brake, hand brakes are provided on the engine and in the guards' vans of a passenger train. These would be called into use only in the remote event of any failure of the automatic brake mechanism.

CHAPTER THE EIGHTH

SLIP-COACH WORKING

I SEE it has now turned twelve o'clock, and we are fast approaching Westbury, where the first slip portion of our train is put off for the Weymouth line. On your left you will soon see the Bratton White Horse, a familiar Great Western Railway landmark out on the Wiltshire Downs and overlooking Westbury Station. It was put on record by Gough, the historian, that the Bratton White Horse was cut in the turf to celebrate the victory of Alfred the Great over the Danes in the battle of Ethandun, A.D. 878.

As we are to "slip" a coach, a short description of the slipping process will not be out of place. When the train is made up, the "slip" coach or coaches, and possibly ordinary coaching stock forming trailers, are placed in the rear, and the slipping apparatus between the "slip" and the main train portion is coupled up as in the illustration. The operation of slipping is performed by means of a lever by a Slip Guard who rides in the front vehicle of the section slipped, the apparatus being fixed in his compartment. The release hook of the "slip" is hinged on a pin and retained in its normal position by means of a sliding bar coupled up at one end to the lever,

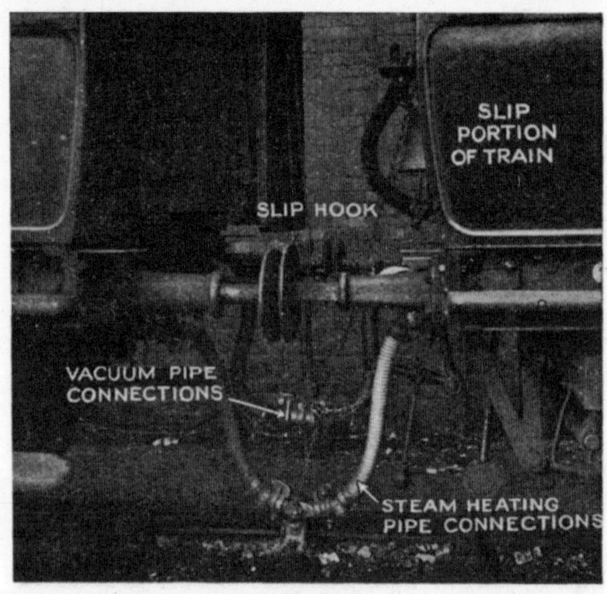

Slip Gear

and the other end of which rests and bears on the hinged portion of the hook. The lever has three positions—"Main Train," the running position; "Slip and Brake On," and "Release," and is connected to and controls a large three-way plug cock situated in the vacuum brake system, containing ports connecting to the train pipe, brake cylinder, reservoir, and the atmosphere. A non-return valve is fitted between this cock and the reservoir.

Between the vacuum brake couplings are fitted two adaptors, secured to them by pins and lugs, the bodies of which, when together, form a coupling capable of being pulled apart with no damage to either. Contained in the adaptor fitted to the coupling of the main train portion is a small valve, which, when closed, seals the train pipe. This valve is held open when the gear is coupled by a cross member in the adjacent adaptor fitted to the "slip" portion, and, when the gear is disconnected, automatically closes.

The screw coupling and flexible connections of the vacuum system are prevented from falling away after the "slip" has been made by chains. Collapsible brackets and chains are used on the steam-heating connections, holding them in position.

On nearing the place where the "slip" is to be made, the driver, if necessary, slightly reduces speed, and the guard of the "slip" pulls the lever right back to the "Slip and Brake On" position. This causes the sliding bar to come away from the drop portion of the release hook, permitting it to fall, leaving the shackle of the screw coupling free to fall also, thus disconnecting the draw-bars and causing the slip portion immediately to fall away from the main portion of the train.

The vacuum brake and train-heating connections are pulled apart, the main train portion of the former, and both portions of the latter, automatically sealing. With the lever in this position, the three-way cock is admitting air to the brake cylinder, so applying the brake on the slip portion. Speed is thus reduced slightly, and, the train portion having proceeded, the guard places the lever in the " middle " or " release " position, connection between the atmosphere and the brake cylinder is closed, and connection between the brake cylinder and

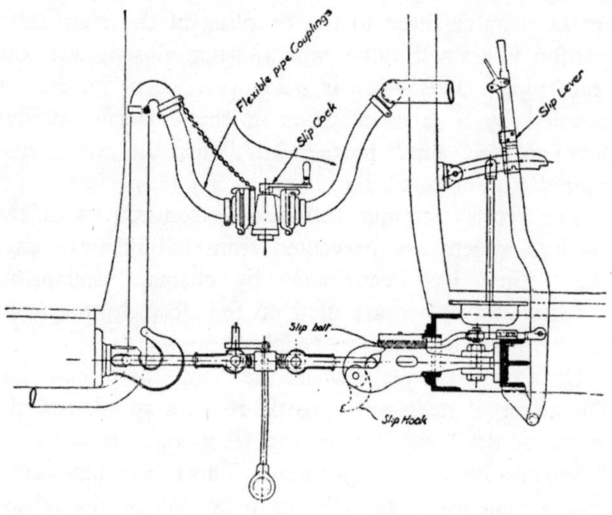

large reservoir established. Air rushing from the former to the latter releases the brake. The guard can then apply or release the brake at will until the vacuum in the reservoirs is destroyed. The capacity of these reservoirs is such that at least three separate applications of the brake can be made.

Having exhausted the vacuum, the guard cannot restore it, and consequently skill and judgment is

ENGINE HEAD SIGNALS

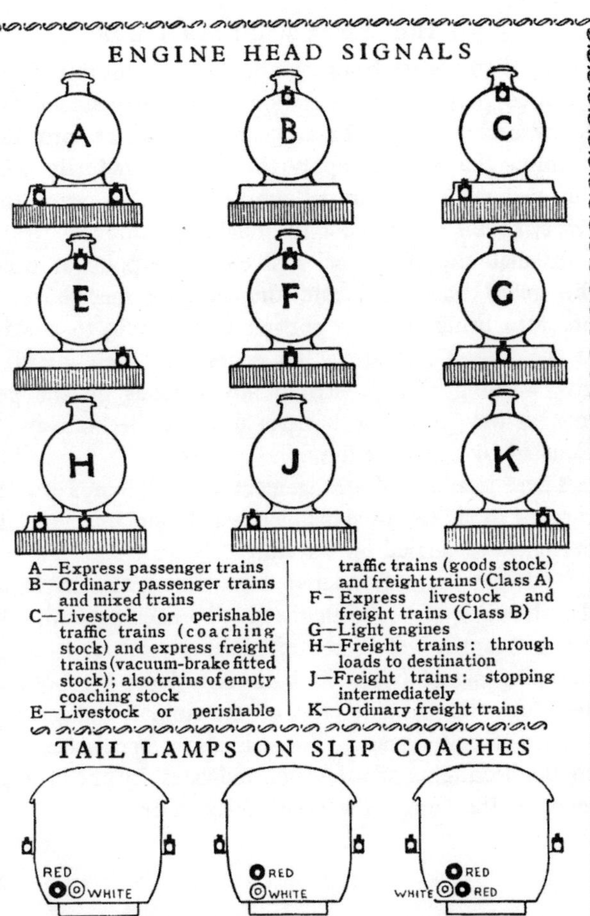

A—Express passenger trains
B—Ordinary passenger trains and mixed trains
C—Livestock or perishable traffic trains (coaching stock) and express freight trains (vacuum-brake fitted stock); also trains of empty coaching stock
E—Livestock or perishable traffic trains (goods stock) and freight trains (Class A)
F—Express livestock and freight trains (Class B)
G—Light engines
H—Freight trains: through loads to destination
J—Freight trains: stopping intermediately
K—Ordinary freight trains

TAIL LAMPS ON SLIP COACHES

RED
WHITE

Lamps carried on a single slip portion, or the last slip portion of a train to be put off.

RED
WHITE

Lamps carried on a second slip portion, i.e., the first of two slips to be put off.

When three slip portions are carried, these lamps are on the second slip.

RED
WHITE RED

Lamps carried on the last of three slips, i.e., the first slip portion to be put off.

required to ensure bringing the "slip" to rest at the required position at the station. An independent hand screw control of the brake gear is, however, provided, enabling the guard to apply the brakes gradually without using the "vacuum" portion of the gear, thus reserving his vacuum for the final application.

A small slipping signal is fixed at the point at which the guard has to operate the slipping mechanism in order to bring the slip portion of the train to a stand at the station platform. To enable the slip guard to give warning of approach to any persons on the permanent way, a motor horn is fitted in his van and is actuated by a foot bellows.

There is a special arrangement of tail lamps on slip coaches to signify to signalmen when one or more slip portions are carried on a train.

You may have wondered how the signalman knows the character of the train that is approaching him. He has a "tapper" bell communicating with each of the adjoining signal boxes in both directions, for both up and down lines. The class of the train is indicated by a code of bell signals. There is also a special series of engine headlights in use which indicates, by the arrangement of the lamps, the class of the train.

CHAPTER THE NINTH

THE PERMANENT WAY

HAVING briefly considered the locomotives and other rolling stock, perhaps we ought to turn our attention for a little while to the railroad itself. What is known as the "permanent way" may be defined as that portion of the railway which lies between the levelled surface of the ground and the upper surface of the rails. The permanent way over which we are now travelling is generally admitted to be one of the finest in the world, and, although we are running at about sixty miles an hour, you will observe that there is an almost entire lack of vibration.

Perhaps you are unaware that the permanent way of the Great Western Railway was originally of broad (7 ft. 0¼ in.) gauge, this gauge having been selected on the recommendation of Brunel, who apparently assumed in those early days of railways that the country would be divided up into railway districts between which it did not appear likely there would be any intercommunication. He was doubtless of the opinion that

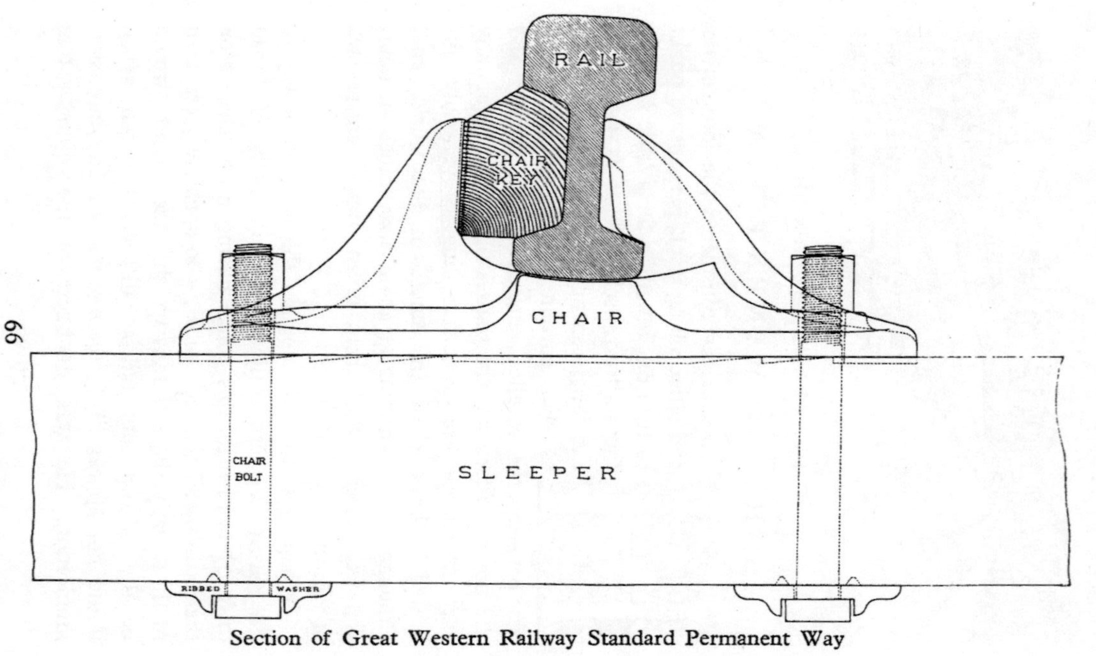

Section of Great Western Railway Standard Permanent Way

higher speeds and bigger loads would be possible on the broad gauge, with steadier and smoother running.

What was known as the "Battle of the Gauges" was waged for some years, and whilst there is little doubt that the broad gauge had much to recommend it and many highly qualified engineers came forward to support Brunel's selection, lines of narrow gauge had been constructed to a considerable extent in the country, and in the end the narrow, or what is now the standard, gauge (4 ft. 8½ ins.) won the day. Conversions from broad to mixed (broad and narrow) or standard gauges were made from 1858 onwards on the Great Western Railway, and the final conversion to standard gauge—a wonderful achievement of engineering—was carried out on May 21 and 22, 1892.

Perhaps you have wondered why the standard gauge was fixed at 4 ft. 8½ ins., and not 4 ft. 6 ins., or 5 ft., for 4 ft. 8½ ins. is certainly an odd sort of measurement. I think, however, this was possibly the gauge of early cart-road tracks which were converted to railways before the advent of steam traction. One railway probably followed the gauge of another until a standard measurement was gradually evolved.

You will probably be more or less familiar with the general construction of the permanent way, and it will here suffice to say that it consists of about twelve inches of "ballast," such as gravel or slag, which is placed upon the firm hard road (formation level). On the ballast rest the sleepers, which are creosoted timbers, 9 ft. long, 10 ins. broad, and 5 ins. deep. These are generally placed about 2 ft. 6½ ins. apart and carry the cast-iron "chairs," which are approximately 15½ ins. by 7½ ins. at base and 52 lbs. in weight. The chairs are secured to the sleepers by bolts and the rails are fixed in the chairs by means of oak blocks known as "keys." The rails incline slightly towards one another. The Great Western standard main line rails weigh 97½ lbs. to the lineal yard. The rails are about 44 ft. 6 ins. in length, and the ends are joined by means of "fish-plates," weighing 33 lbs. per pair, bolted through the rails. You may have noticed that a small space is left between the ends of the rails, generally from a quarter to half an inch. This is to allow for expansion due to heat.

The sectional diagram will explain more clearly than any verbal description the various features of permanent way construction. It should, perhaps, be stated that on curves the outer rail is raised above the level of the inner to reduce friction caused by centrifugal force and to ensure stability of the trains when travelling at high speed. The gradients or variations in the rail level are denoted by the number of lineal feet in which the line rises or falls one foot, and boards indicating the gradients are fixed at the side of the rails for the guidance of engine-drivers and others. The gradients on our journey between Paddington and Plymouth are shewn in this diagram.

At suitable places along the permanent way, Post Office mail-bag apparatus is provided. This consists of a "wayside net" fixed to the ground, which receives bags of mails suspended from an arm extended from the side of a mail van, and a "wayside standard"

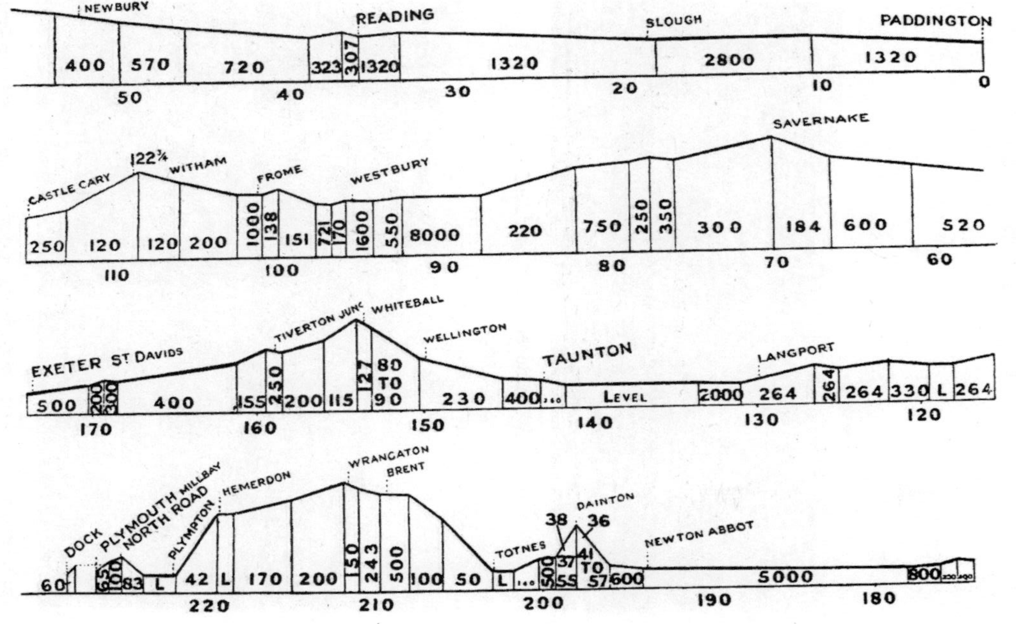

NEWBURY
READING
SLOUGH
PADDINGTON
SAVERNAKE
CASTLE CARY
122¾
WITHAM
FROME
WESTBURY
EXETER ST DAVIDS
TIVERTON JUNC
WHITEBALL
WELLINGTON
TAUNTON
LEVEL
LANGPORT
DOCK
PLYMOUTH MILLBAY
NORTH ROAD
PLYMPTON
HEMERDON
WRANGATON
BRENT
TOTNES
DAINTON
NEWTON ABBOT

Wayside Net and Standard

Train dropping mails in wayside net and picking up from standard

erected from the ground on which mail bags are hung and projected into the mail van by a net extended from the side of the van. In some instances a combination of the two, the net and the standard, is provided.

By this means Post Office mails are put off from the train into the nets and collected from the standards whilst the train is running at speed. These photographs illustrate the apparatus.

The construction of the permanent way involves the provision of embankments, cuttings, over and under bridges, tunnels, viaducts, etc.

There was in the old days a large number of wonderful timbered viaducts on the Great Western Railway, and these have been very largely replaced by steel and stone structures. Just after we leave our train at Plymouth it will pass over the famous Saltash Bridge across the Tamar, one of Brunel's masterpieces of engineering. The bridge consists of nineteen spans, and the total length is 2,200 feet.

The Great Western Railway also comprises the famous Severn Tunnel—the longest underwater railway tunnel in the world. This is not on our line of route to-day, but you may be interested to know that it has a length of 4 miles 620 yards. It took over thirteen years to construct, and was opened for traffic in 1886. It attains a depth of 30 feet below the deepest part of the river bed. It is on record that 76,400,000 bricks and 36,794 tons of cement were used in the construction of the tunnel and its approaches.

You have been assimilating a good deal of food for thought, and I think the time has arrived when we should do something to replenish the "inner boy." I suggest we continue our talk in the restaurant car, where luncheon is now being served.

You will see from the bill of fare that we have a choice of two menus, at 2*s.* 6*d.* and 3*s.* respectively, whilst for children under twelve years of age the charge is 1*s.* 6*d.* each only. These excellent though low-priced luncheons have proved a popular innovation and are another example of the progressive policy of the Great Western Railway.

From your seat in the car you get an undisturbed view of the surrounding country. If you will look alongside the permanent way, you will notice that every now and then we pass a small white post.* These are the quarter-mile posts which indicate the distance from Paddington. They will give us the opportunity of testing our speed and the smoothness of running. If you will take the bottle of ginger-beer you have before you and fill your glass, I will do likewise. We will place the glasses one at each end of our table. I will give you my stop watch and will call out the quarter-mile posts as we pass. I want you to notify me when one minute is up. On sighting the first post I will say, "Go!" and I want you to start the watch. . . . "Go! —One—two—three—four—five (minute up)." You see

* *The quarter-mile posts are placed some on the Up Line and some on the Down Line on the Great Western Railway.*

we have passed five quarter-mile posts in the minute, which means that we have been travelling at the rate of about one mile in forty-eight seconds, or seventy-five miles per hour, but such is the lack of vibration that not one drop has been spilt from either of our glasses. I think you will agree that this is a fairly good test of the smooth running of the coaches on the Great Western Railway. Good health !

Here is a table which will enable you readily to ascertain the speed of trains in miles per hour by taking the time occupied in seconds in travelling between any two consecutive quarter-mile posts.

Time in seconds between quarter-mile posts	*Speed of train—Miles per hour*	*Time in seconds between quarter-mile posts*	*Speed of train—Miles per hour*
10	90	21	42·8
11	81·81	22	40·9
12	75	23	39·11
13	69·2	24	37·5
14	64·28	25	36
15	60	26	34·6
16	56·2	27	33·3
17	52·9	28	32·1
18	50	29	31
19	47·4	30	30
20	45		

NOTE : *Nine hundred, divided by the number of seconds occupied by a train travelling between any two quarter-mile posts, will give you the speed of the train in miles per hour.*

On the question of smooth running, you may be interested to hear of a little incident which occurred at

Kingswear Station. A porter there dropped half a crown as the Torquay express was leaving the station. Search for the coin proved unsuccessful, but it was eventually found on the spring-box of one of the coaches which had in the meantime made a journey from Kingswear to Paddington and back and a local journey from Kingswear to Newton Abbot and back, comprising in all a distance of somewhere about 450 miles!

With this I will leave you to finish your lunch in peace, after which we will have a talk about railway signalling.

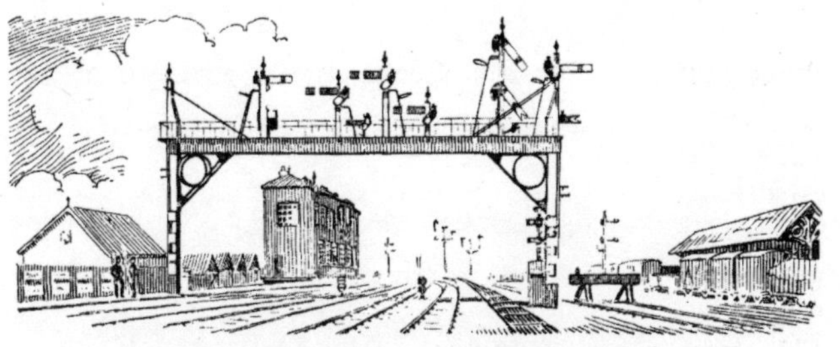

CHAPTER THE TENTH

SIGNALS

PERHAPS one of the most fascinating phases of railway practice is the process by which the trains are controlled along the railway, and the story of railway signalling, which is the story of the evolution of safety appliances on railways, is one of continuous improvement and resultant increase in the safety of railway travel.

One of the earliest features of interest in connection with the control of trains was the first working telegraph of any length, which was installed between Paddington and West Drayton Stations and afterwards extended to Slough. This appliance was used for advising the departure and arrival of trains, and records exist of distinguished visitors having visited Paddington and Slough from time to time to view this wonder of the age, which obtained a good deal of publicity in 1845 through the prompt arrest by its assistance of a murderer travelling on the railway.

The first fixed signals in use were of very primitive character and the earliest signal lamps were merely stable lanterns. To Mr. Cooke, the co-inventor of the

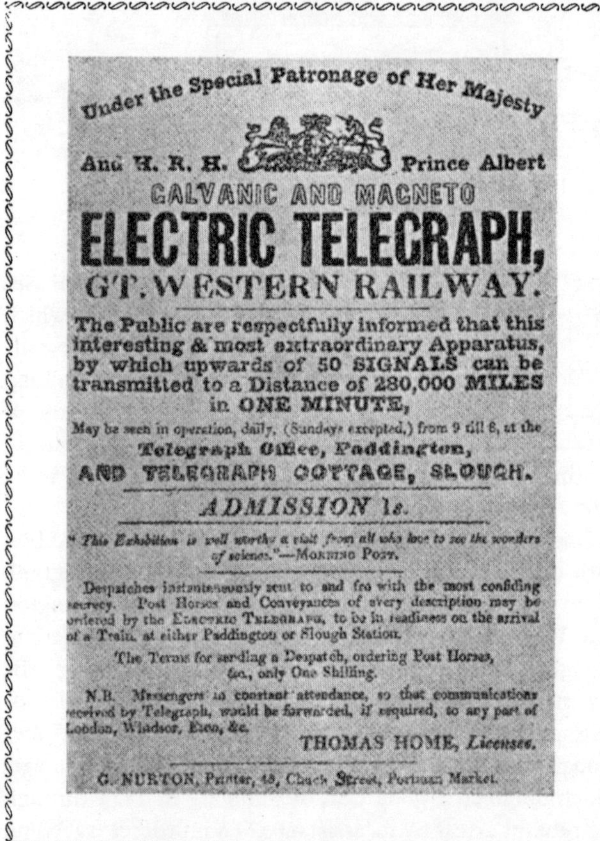

electric telegraph, is due the credit of having realised the possibilities of the telegraph in combination with fixed signals for working trains on the "block" system, i.e. by dividing the line into a number of lengths and allowing only one train at a time to be on the same length of railway. Hitherto, it had been the practice for trains to proceed along the line on a time interval system. The "block" system was first introduced for working trains through tunnels, and whilst then somewhat crude in its application as compared with modern practice, the principles of the "block" system remain to-day.

A considerable advance in signal practice took place with the appointment in 1845 of Mr. C. E. Spagnoletti as Telegraph Superintendent of the Great Western Railway. Mr. Spagnoletti was the inventor of the improved form of three-position disc telegraph instruments which are still in general use throughout the railway.

The semaphore arm type of fixed signal, with which you will be familiar and which has been universally adopted, was introduced in the early 'sixties, and in its first decade was a three-position signal giving indications for "DANGER," "CAUTION," and "ALL RIGHT." The Great Western Railway was one of the first railways to adopt the two-position signal, the "Danger" postiion being indicated by the arm at right angles to the post, and the "All right" indication shewn by the arm at an angle of about 60 degrees.

You will observe that the signal posts on the Great Western Railway are generally placed on the left-hand side of the line as viewed by the driver on the engine footplate. The signal arms, which are painted in red with a white stripe as seen by the engine-driver and white with black stripe on the reverse side, are on the left-hand side of the signal posts. Attached to the signal posts are cases containing lamps which, on the Great Western Railway, are burning continuously day and night (except when being trimmed and cleaned). A special form of lamp economical in oil consumption has been adopted, which requires attention and replenishing with oil about once a week only. To the signal arms are attached coloured spectacles through which the light of the lamps is viewed by the oncoming engine-drivers. When the arm is in the " All right " or " Off " position, a green light is seen, and when in the " Danger " or " On " position, a red light shews. There is a small white back-light which shews in the opposite direction as an indication to the signalman that the signal arm is working and that the lamp is burning.

The movement of trains on railways is controlled by signalmen stationed in signal boxes having signals worked by levers and suitable connections, and electrical instruments for communication with the signal boxes on either side.

The signal boxes are so placed that the line of railway is more or less divided up into equal intervals of space known as block sections, which are protected by signals.

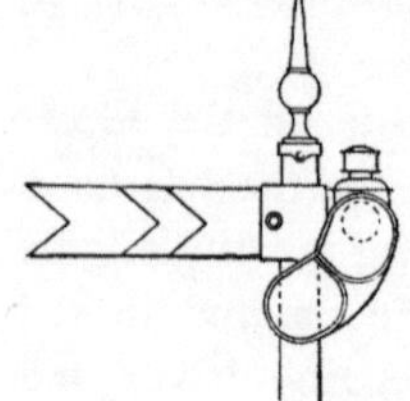

The normal position of all signals is at " Danger."

The DISTANT SIGNAL is a " Caution " signal only, and it is the first signal to be reached by a train approaching a signal box. It is distinguished from all other signals by its arm being fish-tailed. It gives information to a driver as to the state of the line ahead, and it is the only signal which can be passed by a train when it is in the horizontal or " Caution " position. It is fixed at such a distance from the next signal ahead that when it is at " Caution " a driver has sufficient time to bring his train under control in order to stop on reaching the home signal (i.e. about a thousand yards on a falling gradient, eight hundred yards on the level, and six hundred yards on a rising gradient). When the signal is at " All right," the driver knows that he can continue to run at his usual speed and that he will find all the other signals for the section controlled by the distant signal in the " All right " position.

At terminal stations and at places where a speed restriction is imposed, such as on curves, the distant signal is permanently in the " Caution " position and cannot be lowered by the signalman.

You will realise that at night there is little to enable the engine-driver to distinguish distant signals from others beyond his knowledge of the road and the position of one signal in relation to others. In order to remedy this the Great Western Railway have adopted an amber light experimentally for distant signals, and where this has been done the arms of distant signals are painted amber instead of red.

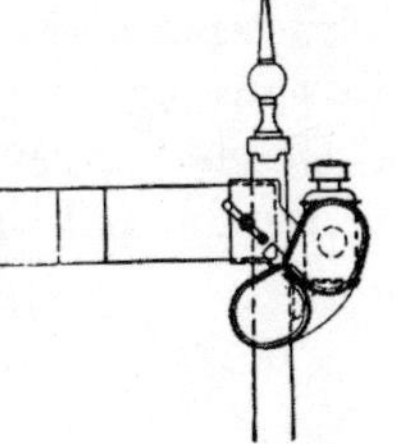

The HOME SIGNAL is the second signal reached and is usually near a signal box. It is a stop signal and must not be passed at " Danger." Its function when " On " is to stop a train clear of any junctions there may be with other lines, and also clear of the next section ahead.

The STARTING SIGNAL is the third signal reached, and is placed in such a position that any operations which may have to be performed at the signal box can be carried out without having to pass this signal, which controls the entrance of a train into the next section ahead. In some cases an ADVANCED STARTING SIGNAL is provided about a train's length or so ahead of the starting signal, e.g. when there is a cross-over road or other points ahead of the starting signal.

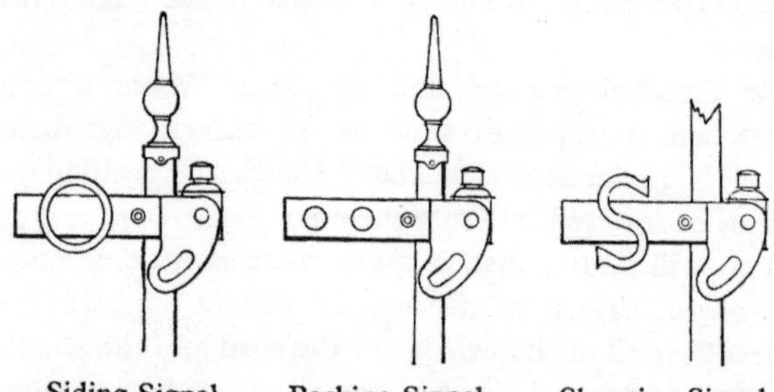

Siding Signal　　Backing Signal　　Shunting Signal

There are many other signals which are used for various purposes, such as shunting, backing, etc., and these have distinguishing indications, as illustrated.

On our journey from Paddington to Plymouth we pass 68 stations and no fewer than 523 signals.

CHAPTER THE ELEVENTH

HOW TRAINS ARE CONTROLLED

It is now necessary to describe briefly how signalmen are enabled to control the trains along the railway. This is done by means of the electrical instruments already referred to. The signalmen can also generally communicate with one another by telephone.

Each signal box is provided with a tapper bell for each section on either side for both " Up " and " Down " lines, on which are sent and received, by means of a code, the bell signals relative to a train requiring to pass through those sections.

Tapper Bell

We will imagine that three signal boxes on the line of route of a train are occupied by Brown, Jones, and Robinson in the order named.

On receipt of the bell signal " Is line clear ?" from Brown,

Jones has to satisfy himself that there is no train in his section and that the line is clear for a distance of a quarter of a mile (the " clearing point ") inside his home signal. If this is the case, Jones repeats the bell signal to Brown's signal box and brings into use his (Jones') key-disc instrument. This instrument has three positions, " Line clear," " Line blocked " (normal), and " Train on line." When a train can be accepted from Brown's signal box, Jones, after sending the bell signal, pegs the key-disc instrument in his signal box to shew " Line clear," and his action simultaneously records " Line clear " in a keyless disc instrument in Brown's signal box. (You will observe that the disc instrument in the box in the rear, being keyless, is under the control of the signalman in the box in advance.) Permission is thus given for the train to be sent forward. Brown, after lowering his starting signal for the train to proceed, at once sends another bell signal to Jones' signal box, " Train entering section." Upon receipt of this, Jones alters his key-disc instrument from " Line clear " by pegging " Train on line," and this indication is also simultaneously shewn in the keyless disc instrument in Brown's box. Jones then, in turn, offers the train to Robinson's box,

Key Disc

and if there is no train in Robinson's section and it is clear up to the standard clearing point, Robinson gives " Line clear " to Jones, pegging his key disc accordingly, which gives the " Line clear " indication on Jones' keyless disc, and so the operation as between Brown's and Jones' signal boxes is repeated between Jones' and Robinson's signal boxes, and in each pair of signal boxes along the line as the train advances.

Keyless Disc

When the train arrives at Jones' signal box and is found to be complete (which fact is known by all trains carrying a red " tail lamp "—illuminated at night—on the last vehicle), Jones, having replaced his distant, home, and starting signals to " danger," sends a bell signal to Brown, " Train out of section," and unpegs his key-disc instrument from " Train on line," which then shews the normal indication which means " Line blocked."

The same processes are gone through with regard to trains on both " Up " and " Down " lines, and you will now realise how these operations ensure that only one train can be in one section on the same line at one time.

Where sections are very short (as at junctions), the " Is line clear ? " signal has to be sent forward as soon as it has been acknowledged to the signal box in the rear. When the next signal box in advance is within a quarter of a mile of the home signal in rear, the signalman in advance must not give "Line clear" to the signal

box in rear until "Train out of section" for the previous train has been received from the next signal box ahead.

It is obvious that on busy sections of line, where the distance between signal boxes is short, a fast train would be slowing down every minute or two whilst "Line clear" was being obtained. The "Train approach" signal, however, enables several sections to be cleared ahead so as to ensure a clear line, and every time a certain signal box is reached in the chain of boxes the signalman starts the "Train approach" signal, so that a further section of the line is prepared to allow of the passage of the train. Example:

A. B. C. D. E. F. G. H. I. J. K. L. M. N. O. P.

FIRST GROUP SECOND GROUP THIRD GROUP

"Line clear" has been obtained from signal boxes A. to D. When the train reaches C., the "Train approach" signal is passed to E., who starts "Line clear" for another chain of signal boxes stopping at J. At H., the "Train approach" signal is given again, and so on.

This is briefly the normal procedure in passing a train along an ordinary double line of railway when no obstruction exists.

Signalmen are assisted in their duties by numerous appliances designed with a view to safe working. One of the most important of these is, perhaps, what is known as "Track Circuiting," of which the following is a brief description. A length of railway line is insulated to form a complete electrical circuit by having insulated fishplates on the rail joints at each end. The rails between these insulated fishplates are joined together by wire bonds to enable the electric current to be continuous. The electric current is provided by means of a battery fixed at one end, and the current is made to pass through a mechanism called a "relay" at the opposite end of the length of line track circuited. In the signal box is provided an indicator which shews "Track clear" when no train is on the track-circuited portion of line, and is immediately altered to "Track occupied" as soon as a train enters upon the track circuit. By these means a signalman is able to tell when his line is " clear " or

" occupied " by a train, even although the train on line is entirely out of sight. It is also possible for the lever working the signal leading on to the track circuited portion

of line to be electrically locked, so as to prevent an " All right " signal being given when the line is not clear.

Electric " repeaters " are provided in signal boxes for signals which are not visible from the signal box, in order that the signalman may know when the levers

operating the signals have done their work. The arm itself is repeated by a miniature flag in the signal box instrument shewing " On " or " Off," and the signal

lamp by a flag shewing " In ' or " Out." In the case of a lamp failing and the flag showing " Out," a bell is made to ring in order to attract the signalman's attention

CHAPTER
THE TWELFTH

SIGNAL BOX EQUIPMENT

WE will now take a look at the inside of a signal box. Here we see a number of levers arranged in a frame. These are connected with the various signals and points by wires and iron rodding respectively. In order to operate the signals, they are pulled forward or pushed backward in the frame. It should here be noted that the backward position is the normal one in all cases, and when the levers are in that position the signals are

Interior of Signal Box

at danger, and the points set for the main line. The levers are held in position by a catch, which is released by pressing a spring handle when moving the lever forward or backward.

LEVERS are painted in distinctive colours to assist the signalman in his operations, viz., distant signals—green; "stop" signals—red; points or switches—black; facing point locks—blue; spare levers—white, and detonator-laying levers—white, with black bands. The tapper bells, key and keyless discs, telephones and other instruments for communicating with adjoining signal boxes are conveniently arranged on a shelf over the levers, and a "locking diagram" is placed so as to be in full view of the signalman when working the levers and instruments.

The larger and top numbers on the faces of the levers

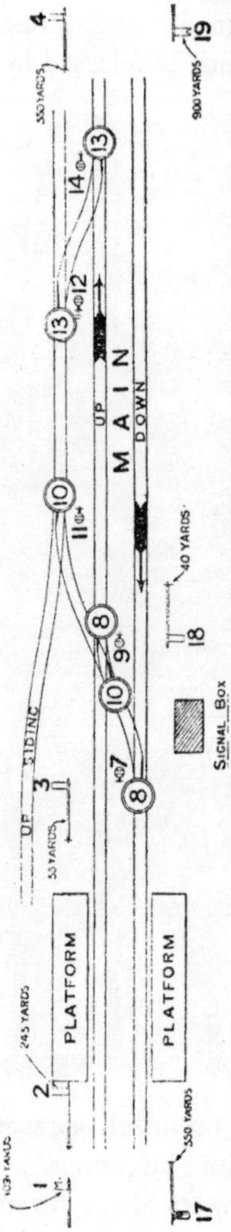

refer to the signals, points, etc., as numbered in the locking diagram. Where other smaller numbers appear on the levers, these refer to the "leads," i.e. the other levers which have, owing to the interlocking of the signals, etc., to be moved before the lever can be released.

POINTS or switches are the means by which a train travels from one set of lines to another. They consist of pairs of movable hinged rails, tapering at their points, inside fixed rails, and are worked from the signal box by rodding supported on roller bearings. The hinged end is termed the "heel" and the thin blade-like end the "toe." When the "toe" faces a train in the running direction the points are called "facing points," and when the train passes over the "heel" first they are termed "trailing points."

COMPENSATORS are provided to counteract any expansion or contraction of the iron rodding.

In some cases small ground signals—called DISC SIGNALS—are provided at points. Five disc signals are shewn in this locking diagram as worked by levers Nos. 7, 9, 11, 12, and 14.

INTERLOCKING means that levers obstruct or free the movements of one another in such a manner as to ensure the correct working of points and signals, and to prevent the exhibition of conflicting signals.

The time at our disposal will not permit of any exhaustive treatise on the interlocking of signals, etc., but from what I have already said you will now be able to appreciate the necessity for the signals being so interlocked that the distant signals cannot be lowered until the home and starting signals have been pulled " off." The " home " and " starting " signals are, therefore, " leads " for the distant signals. In a similar way any points connected with the running lines must be in correct position for the passage of a train before the home or starting signals can be lowered, and this is secured by interlocking between signals and points.

Ground Disc Signal

Each lever is provided with a " tappet " or " tailpiece," which is attached to it and moves backward and forward with the lever. Running at right angles to this tappet, and close to it, either under or above, are the lock bars. These bars in the smaller frames are provided with studs or wedge-shaped pieces, fitted in such a manner as to impede the movement of the tappets when

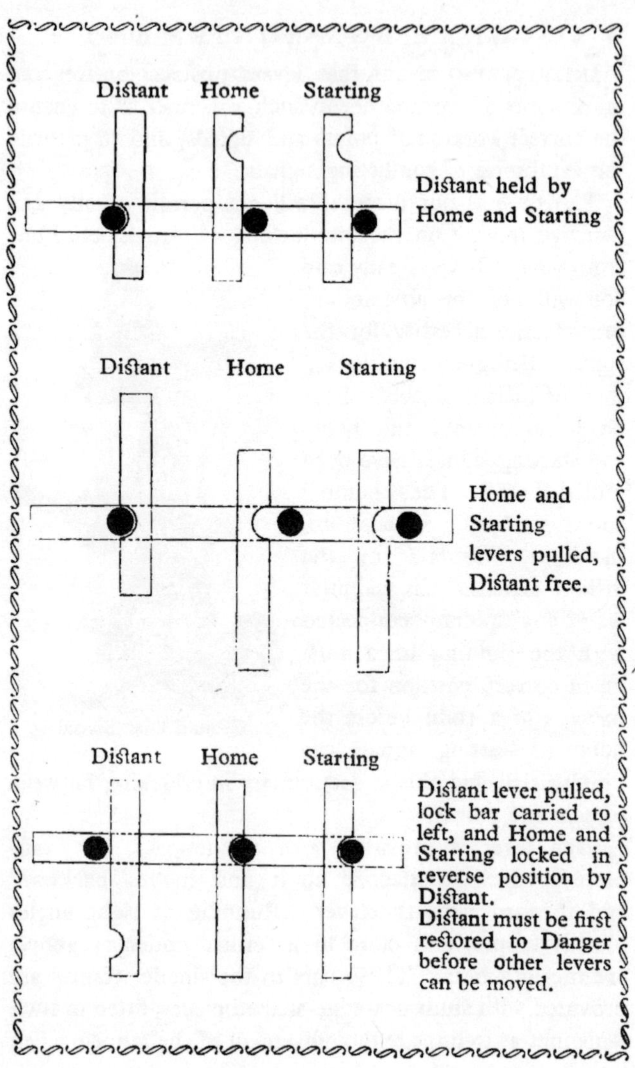
Distant
Home
Starting
Distant held by Home and Starting
Distant
Home
Starting
Home and Starting levers pulled, Distant free.
Distant
Home
Starting
Distant lever pulled, lock bar carried to left, and Home and Starting locked in reverse position by Distant.
Distant must be first restored to Danger before other levers can be moved.

the levers to which the tappets are attached should be locked.

This is perhaps a little involved, but I think it will be made clear if you will carefully study these three simple diagrams, which represent the locking and back-locking which takes place between the distant, home, and starting signals at, say, a small roadside station.

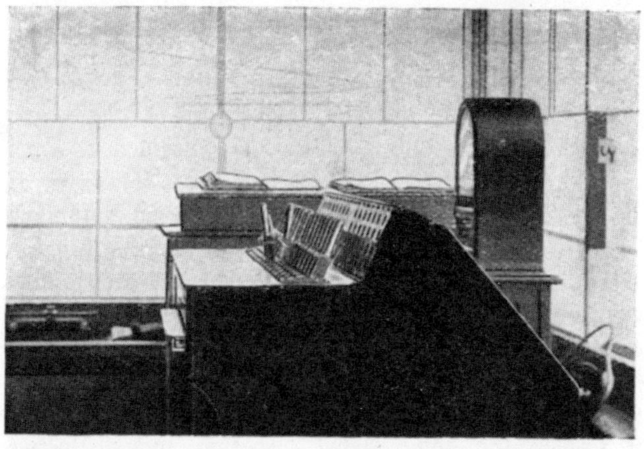

Interlocking methods here described are repeated *ad infinitum* with the locking of all other points and signals in the locking frame.

At some places electric power is used for working points and signals from signal boxes, and some idea of the difference in operation for the signalman may be gained by comparing this photograph with that of the interior of the signal box where ordinary mechanical means are used.

CHAPTER THE THIRTEENTH

SAFETY APPLIANCES

IN their continued efforts to increase the safety of railway travel, the Great Western Railway has installed at some points on its system what is known as the Great Western System of Automatic Control combined with Audible Signals.

The primary object of this system is to give audible warning to an engine-driver when his train is approaching a distant signal in the " On " position, and, in the event of this warning being disregarded, automatically to apply the brakes so as to ensure the train being pulled up before it reaches the home signal. Another and distinctive audible indication is also given on the engine when the distant signal is " Off." The value of this latter indication is that it facilitates the running of the train when the semaphore signals cannot be seen during fogs and snow-storms. The audible signals given are the sounding of a siren indicating " Signal on," and the ringing of a bell indicating " Signal off."

The apparatus fixed on the permanent way for operating the audible signals on the engine is an immovable ramp about 40 feet long between the running rails, consisting of a steel T-bar mounted on a baulk of timber. The ramp at its highest point is four inches above rail-level. A telegraph wire connects the ramp with a switch in

Engine Shoe in contact with Ramp

the signal box. This switch is attached to the lever controlling the distant signal.

The apparatus on the engine comprises a contact shoe, an electrically controlled brake valve and siren combined, and an electric bell. The contact shoe is fixed in the centre line of the engine and projects to within 2½ inches above rail-level. It is capable of being raised vertically, and, being in line with the ramp, it will be seen that it is lifted 1½ inches whenever a ramp is passed over, this lift opening a switch attached to the contact shoe.

The mechanism is adaptable to double or single lines of railway.

You will now have some idea of the precautions which are taken to safeguard trains along the railway in which all other considerations are subservient to that of safety. Before we proceed I ought, perhaps, to emphasise the point that in the event of any failure in any part of the mechanism the signals would go to "danger." For example, signal arms are so weighted that, in the event of breakage of the signal wire, the arms, if "off," would come back into the horizontal position. In addition to the apparatus which has been explained, there is a multitude of additional safety appliances, and I will briefly describe a few of the more important.

Audible Signal in Engine Cab

FACING POINT LOCKS: You will realise that facing points would be a source of danger if not in correct alignment in passing trains, and in order to ensure their proper action, facing point locks and locking bars with detectors are provided at all facing points on passenger lines. The facing point lock consists of a " stretcher blade " joining the two switch blades and pierced with two holes and a plunger, worked by the special lever from the signal box, which passes through one of the

holes in the stretcher blade according to the direction in which the facing points are set, and prevents any movement of the points until the plunger is withdrawn.

The facing point lock lever is interlocked with the home signal, and the latter cannot be lowered until the facing point lock lever has been operated. In order to make security even more secure, another appliance is brought into use, viz., the locking bar.

LOCKING BARS : In order to prevent the signalman withdrawing the plunger whilst the train is actually passing over the points, a bar, sufficiently long to cover the wheel-base of the longest vehicle in use, is fixed inside or outside the rail just to the rear of the facing points. It operates on a series of cranks in such a manner that when moved it rises and falls, and when rising would be stopped by the flanges of any wheels or, if outside the rails, by the wheels themselves passing over the points.

This locking bar is worked by the same lever as the facing point lock, and you will now see that it is quite impossible for the signalman to unbolt the points when a train is passing over them. But there is still an additional safeguard provided in the form of a detector lock.

DETECTOR LOCKS: These locks, as applied to facing points, serve to detect anything wrong with the points in the event of the facing point lock failing to act, and to prevent signals governing such points being lowered until the points are in correct position.

In the event of such remote contingencies as the rodding which connects the facing point lock with the signal box either breaking or being out of adjustment, the stretcher blade breaking, or the points being run through in the trailing direction and damaged, the fact would be discovered by the detector lock.

The main idea of the detector lock is that a blade or some similar device, worked in connection with the points, shall cross the path of another blade or blades worked in connection with the stop signal or signal protecting the points in such a manner that should the points be out of adjustment in any respect, the blade working off the points will form an obstruction to the pulling of the signal wire.

There are various forms of detector locks, but I am afraid time will not permit of a description of them.

FOULING BARS : Where the fouling point between converging tracks cannot clearly be seen from the signal box and there is risk of a signalman giving permission for a movement along one track which is partly obstructed by a vehicle standing on another, " fouling bars " are provided. These are similar in form to and are the same length as facing point locking bars, and are fixed with one end at the actual fouling point. When any vehicle is foul, the bar cannot be moved and thus it prevents a train approaching on the obstructed line.

DETONATOR PLACER MACHINES : In describing the levers in the signal box we mentioned detonator-laying levers. In connection with certain signal boxes detonator " placer " machines have been provided, worked by a lever from the signal box, by means of which the signalman is able to place two detonators on the rail in advance of the home signal for use when the fixed signals are obscured by fog, etc., or in emergencies when it is necessary for the signalman to stop a train. When the detonator " placer " lever is in the normal or forward position, i.e. away from the signalman, the detonators are under cover in an iron casting fixed close to the rail and slightly below rail level, and when the lever in the box is reversed, the detonators are thrust forward upon the rail head.

Two detonator placer levers can be seen at the extreme right of the large photograph of the interior of a signal box which we looked at when discussing signal box equipment.

The mention of detonators brings us to the necessity for their use in railway signalling. The detonator consists of an explosive contained in a round metal case.

Detonator

The detonators are employed to give an audible signal to the driver of a train in case of fog or falling snow or when the fixed signals are not clearly visible. When placed on the rails by hand, detonators are secured by means of lead strips and are exploded by the wheels of an

Detonator in position on Rail

engine passing over them. In order to make sure of getting a report, the regulations provide for two detonators being placed in position, and an ingenious apparatus has been devised, known as the " detonator economiser," which utilises the impact from the explosion of the first detonator to remove the second detonator.

At this point I ought to explain that the arrangements for signalling trains are considerably tightened up during fog or falling snow. Fogmen are stationed at distant signals and place detonators on the line when the signals are in the "Danger" position. Detonator-placing machines which obviate the fogmen going on to the line itself are largely employed for this purpose. The fogmen also exhibit a red hand signal to oncoming engine-drivers. When the distant signal is in the "All right" position the detonators are removed from the line and the fogmen show a green hand signal to the engine-driver. The regulations provide that the absence of a hand signal after the detonator has exploded must be regarded as equal to a "Danger" signal.

At all times during fog, or when the fixed signals are not clearly visible, the speed of trains is reduced and every precaution is taken to ensure that a train may be promptly brought to a stand short of any obstruction.

CHAPTER THE FOURTEENTH

SINGLE LINES OF RAILWAY

So far our chat upon railway signalling has been confined to double lines of railway, as on the route by which we are travelling. You may, however, be interested to know something of the arrangements for signalling on single lines of railway. There are several systems in use of which the principles are the same, and an essential feature is that the engine-driver shall have in his possession some visible evidence of the permission given him by the signalman to bring his train upon a section of single line. The various forms are the " Train Staff," " Train Staff and Ticket;" and the " Electric Staff," " Tablet " or " Token," which I will briefly describe.

The simplest form of single-line working is the train staff system. It applies to short branch lines worked by one engine in steam. The train staff is about the length of and not unlike a policeman's truncheon, and bears upon it the names of the stations at either end. With only one engine in operation, there is obviously no possibility of collision and the staff is simply a visible authority to be upon the line.

SINGLE LINES OF RAILWAY

On single lines where more than one train is operating the line is divided into block sections in the same way as double lines of railway, and the "train staff and ticket," or one of the other systems enumerated, is used. The signalling arrangements are similar to those already described, but the locking at single - line "crossing stations" (places where a short length of double road is provided in order that two trains may pass one another) is so arranged that the Up and Down home signals cannot be "off" at the same time.

Picking-up Post

To enable a staff to be picked up and set down without stopping a train, a loop is provided at the end of the staff, through which the fireman places his arm in picking up. The loop is placed over a horn or hook at the setting-down post, as shewn in these photographs.

You will appreciate that on such single lines it may be necessary for two or more trains to proceed in one direction when there is no intermediate service in the opposite direction, so that after the passage of the first train the train staff is not brought back to the signal box from which it was issued for use for the second train. This is where the "ticket" arrangement comes in, and there is a regulation that no train is permitted to leave a signal box unless the driver is either in *possession* of, or actually *sees* the "staff." Where a second train is to follow in the same direction, the driver of the first train is shewn the "staff" and handed what is known as a "train staff ticket." The tickets, which are kept in a special box at the signal box, cannot be taken out without the train staff, as the key of the box is affixed to the end of the staff. Further, the key cannot be withdrawn unless the box

Setting-down Post

has been locked. The train staff and tickets for each section of the line are of a distinctive pattern.

The electric staff, electric tablet, and electric token systems are all similar in principle, and one or the other are in use where a number of trains may have to run in one direction without an intermediate train in the opposite direction. Instruments containing the staffs, tablets, or tokens are provided for each section of the line.

The combined action of the signalmen at each end of a section is necessary to release a staff, tablet, or token, and only one staff, tablet, or token can be out at a time for any section, so that when (say) a staff has been taken out of an instrument and given to an engine-driver at "A" who is proceeding to "B," a second staff cannot be taken out at "A" until the first has been replaced in the instrument at "B," and then only by the combined action of the two signalmen concerned.

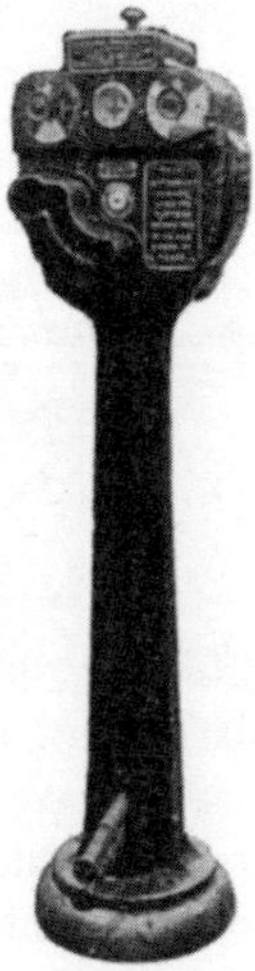

Electric Train Staff Instrument

The electrical mechanism which enables this to be done is quite simple, but I am afraid that detailed descriptions of the operations would be rather lengthy and we have not now time to consider them further.

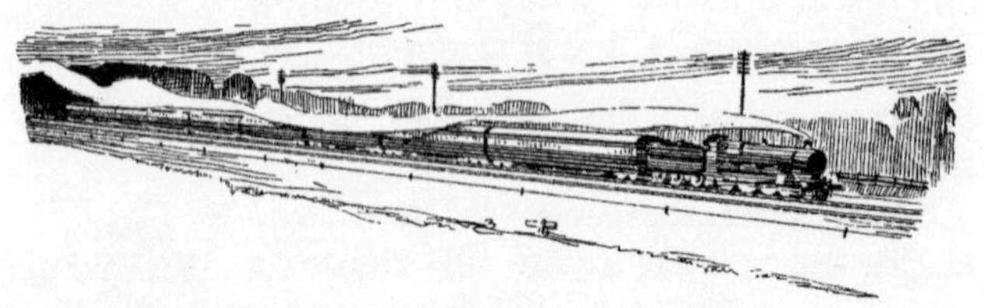

CHAPTER THE FIFTEENTH

TRAIN SPEEDS

THE Great Western Railway has always been noted for its wonderful train speeds. As long ago as 1848 it had trains whose booked time was nearly fifty-seven miles per hour. This was in the old broad gauge days, when loads were about one-sixth of what they are to-day.

You have probably heard something of such famous trains as the "Flying Dutchman," "Zulu," etc. The former, which originated as the 11.45 A.M. from Paddington (Down) and 10.30 A.M. from Exeter (Up), made the journey each way in four and a half hours, with stops at Didcot, Swindon, Bath, Bristol, and Taunton. The timing of this train was fifty-seven minutes to Didcot, about 53 miles, but by this time the coaches were bigger and the loads heavier than in the "forties." The "Zulu" (3 P.M. from Paddington), put on in 1880, was timed to Exeter in four and a quarter hours—just eight minutes longer than our train takes to-day to run to Plymouth—about thirty-two miles farther.

The year 1904 was marked by the innovation of a non-stop train, down and up, between Paddington and Plymouth (North Road), 245½ miles, which was then and still is the longest run of the kind in the world by daily or regular trains. From the thirty-sixth mile to about the hundred and seventieth mile the speed was slightly over sixty miles an hour. The time allowed from Paddington to Plymouth was four hours, twenty-five minutes. This train originally left Paddington at 10.10 A.M. on the "down" journey, and Penzance at 10.10 A.M. on the "up" journey. For two years it ran in the summer season only. It was the forerunner of the train in which you are now travelling, the celebrated "Cornish Riviera Limited Express." The remarkable schedule of the train in 1904 is given below, and it should be noted that this was before the shortened route through Castle Cary (by which we are travelling) was opened in 1906, effecting a saving of nineteen miles.

DISTANCE		TIMES FROM PADDINGTON			
Miles	Chains			Hrs.	Mins.
		PADDINGTON - - - - -	*dep.*		—
24	21	Maidenhead - - - - -	*pass*	0	25½
36	0	Reading - - - - - -	,,	0	36
53	9	Didcot - - - - - -	,,	0	53
77	21	Swindon - - - - - -	,,	1	17
93	77	Chippenham - - - - -	,,	1	33
106	70	*Bath - - - - - -	,,	1	46
116	78	*East Depot (Bristol) - -	,,	1	56
117	42	*Bristol (Marsh Junction) -	,,	1	58
118	33	* ,, (Pyle Hill Junction) -	,,	2	0
162	67	Taunton - - - - - -	,,	2	43
169	73	Wellington - - - - -	,,	2	49½
173	50	Whiteball Siding - - -	,,	†2	54½
193	50	*Exeter (St. David's) - -	,,	3	15
		(Single line tablet slacks: *Dawlish)			
		*Dawlish (Tunnel Box) - -	,,		—
213	65	*Newton Abbot - - - -	,,	3	40½
245	53	NORTH ROAD, PLYMOUTH -	*arr.*	4	25

* *Service slacks.* † *About.*

When slip coaches for Taunton and Exeter were put on the down train, Taunton was brought within two hours, twenty-nine minutes of London (142⅞ miles).

The record non-stop regular run Paddington to Plymouth has now stood unassailed for nearly twenty years.

It is not, perhaps, generally known that during the past twenty-five years the Great Western Railway has constructed about 100 miles of new main line—about the distance from London to Bath—in order to improve its train services. Here is a list of some of the fastest Great Western trains:

	DISTANCE Miles	TIME Mins.	AVERAGE SPEED M.P.H.
Swindon–London - - - -	77¼	75	61·8
Paddington–Bath - - - - -	107	105	61·1
Paddington–Bristol (*via* Bath) - -	118¼	120	59·1
Bristol–Paddington (*via* Badminton)	117½	120	58·7
Paddington–Westbury - - -	95½	97	59
Paddington–Exeter - - - -	173¾	180	57·9
Banbury–Paddington - - - -	67½	70	57·8
Paddington–Leamington - - -	87¼	90	58·1
Leamington–High Wycombe - -	60¾	63	57·8
Paddington–Taunton - - - -	143	148	57·97
Paddington–Torquay - - - -	199¾	215	55·7
Paddington–Plymouth - - -	225¾	247	54·8
Paddington–Birmingham - - -	110½	120	55·2

These are not all single trains. There are two trains doing the Bath run in 105 minutes daily, and there are four two-hour expresses between London and Bristol. The fast runs by the down trains to Torquay, Exeter, and Taunton are balanced by equally expeditious travelling on the up journeys.

The run from Swindon to Paddington (2.30 P.M. train from Cheltenham), 77¼ miles in seventy-five minutes, giving an average speed of 61·8 miles an hour, is the fastest booked "start to stop" run in the British Isles.

So far, we have only looked at regular booked timings. There have been some really remarkable *special* runs, but we cannot here refer to more than one, when the highest authoritative speed recorded on any British Railway, viz., 102·3 miles per hour, was achieved. The timing was taken by the late Mr. C. Rous-Marten, a recognised authority on locomotive performances, and he took a systematic instrumental record of the speed. Subsequently he sought permission from the General Manager, Mr. (afterwards Sir) James Inglis, to publish the record, but for various reasons the permission was withheld, and consequently the full particulars remained secret for many years.

The complete story is told in the following communication, which was made by Mr. Rous-Marten to Mr. James Inglis on June 20, 1905:

DEAR MR. INGLIS: Pursuant to my recent letter and in accordance with the suggestion in your letter of the 7th instant, I now "take up the correspondence at the point at which it ceased" relative to the question of publishing the maximum speed in your record run of May, 1904.

First, let me state my own side of the case—The Great Western is wooing public favour and, very properly, seeking to increase traffic to the Far West by means of extra-fast non-stopping trains. Now, I happened last year to hear a good deal of conversation with reference in particular to those Paddington-Plymouth non-stop runs. To my surprise, many people of different ages, sexes, and callings declared that nothing would induce them to travel by trains which ran at such "fearful speeds." Whenever opportunity decently offered, I "cut in" and pointed out that in reality these trains did not run, or need to run, nearly so fast as many other Great Western trains which had been running unnoticed for a number of years, and that the time was gained, not through extra speeds, but through lighter loads and absence of stops. This was received with a good deal of incredulity, but when I proved my case, first by the actual figures, and secondly by the proof (although of course without giving the actual maximum) that with the Ocean Specials I had on more than one occasion recorded speeds enormously higher than the fastest that are run by the trains in question, and that at these times the travelling was the smoothest, easiest, and therefore safest of any, I was able to compel conviction.

Now this is the basis of my proposal, that the maximum attained by these non-passenger-carrying specials, which was from 30 to 50 per cent. higher than that run by those best regular long-distance expresses, should now be made public *pour encourager les autres*, or at any rate to make the travelling public see that when going by your best regular trains they will not run at a rate at all approaching that which has been attained with perfect ease and safety by non-passenger or experimental specials.

You have doubtless noticed letters in the papers referring to " terrific " or " dangerous " speed being run by regular expresses, such as " 70 to 80 miles an hour." But the Record Mail Special averaged 70·2 from the Exeter " slow pass " to the Bristol stop, and 71·5 from the Bristol start to the Paddington stop, notwithstanding the delays of the Bath service-slack and the very bad special slow over the Cricklade bridge under repair, while between Swindon and Paddington we maintained a steady average of 80 miles an hour for 73 miles on end.

These facts have, of course, been published already; indeed, could be readily gathered from the published log of the train. The actual maximum rate has not, so far, got into print. Indeed, I am not aware that anybody but myself recorded it with absolute accuracy, although I suspect that one of the Post Office people must have done some timing, for he came very near the truth in that Plymouth paper's article which I sent you, and which gives an illustration of " *City of Truro* averaging 99 to 100 miles an hour." But, of course, a mere statement in a daily newspaper carries but little weight.

Confidential.—In now giving you my actual figures, it is, I

THE LOG OF THE TRAIN

Distance	*Stations*	*Arrive*	*Depart*	*Time occupied*	*Speed per hour*
m. ch.		h. m. s.	h. m. s.	m. s.	miles
	Plymouth: Mill Bay Crossing	—	a.m. 9 23 10	— —	—
23 79	Totnes . . .	—	9 50 49	27 39	52.05
8 55	Newton Abbot	—	9 59 52	9 3	57.59
20 15	Exeter . . .	—	10 22 12	22 20	54.23
30 63	Taunton . .	—	10 50 1	27 49	66.41
11 45	Bridgwater .	—	10 59 24	9 23	73.94
32 69	Bristol: Pylle Hill .	11 26 29	11 30 12	27 5	72.80
1 35	East Depot .	—	11 33 51	3 39	23.63
10 9	Bath . . .	—	11 43 50	9 59	60.78
29 48	Swindon . .	—	p.m. 12 9 49	25 59	68.35
24 13	Didcot . . .	—	12 29 20	19 31	74.28
17 9	Reading . . .	—	12 42 21	13 1	78.88
36 0	Paddington—platform .	1 9 38	—	27 17 From Reading	79.17
	dead stop .	1 9 58	—	27 37	—

	h. m. s.
Total time occupied: Paddington platform .	3 46 28
„ dead stop .	3 46 48

Speed per hour throughout, including stops . 65.49 miles

Speed per hour throughout, excluding stops . 66.39 miles

Load of 8-wheeled vans from Plymouth . . 5

Load of 8-wheeled vans from Bristol . . . 4

Engines and Drivers:

Plymouth to Bristol, No. 3440, "City of Truro," Driver Clements.

Bristol to Paddington, No. 3065, "Duke of Connaught," Driver Underhill.

feel sure, unnecessary for me to stipulate that they shall be regarded as strictly confidential, and that in no case shall my information be used to anybody's prejudice. Upon that I am quite certain I can depend without any specific pledge on your part.

What happened was this: when we topped the Whiteball Summit, we were still doing 63 miles an hour; when we emerged from the Whiteball Tunnel we had reached 80; thenceforward our velocity rapidly and steadily increased, the quarter-mile times diminishing from 11 secs. at the tunnel entrance to 10·6 secs., 10·2 secs., 10 secs., 9·8 secs., 9·4 secs., 9·2 secs., and finally to 8·8 secs., this last being equivalent to a rate of 102·3 miles an hour. The two quickest quarters thus occupied exactly 18 secs. for the half-mile, equal to 100 miles an hour. At this time the travelling was so curiously smooth that, but for the sound, it was difficult to believe we were moving at all, and the perfect control retained over the train was strikingly manifested through what appeared at the time the vexatious incident of those platelayers dawdling on the 4-ft. way, which compelled a sudden reduction of the speed by about one-half, which was effected in the readiest and simplest way conceivable, without the slightest jerk or irregularity.

And now "the murder is out"! It seems to me to afford a strong argument for the consolation of the timid folk who might otherwise be deterred from enjoying the comfort and celerity of your splendid expresses, to be able to impress upon them that at the highest speed they would travel they would be going quite slowly compared with that at which the mail-special ran with entire ease and safety. I hope you will agree with me in this opinion.

I am, yours very sincerely,

C. Rous-Marten

Eldon Chambers,
30 Fleet Street, E.C.

"One hundred miles per hour" and "the travelling so curiously smooth that it was difficult to believe we were moving at all"! No wonder the Great Western Railway is referred to as

"The Line that put the 'ees' in spEEd"

CHAPTER THE SIXTEENTH

FREIGHT TRAINS

OUR time is going and we shall soon be at our destination, so I am afraid there is much about railway operation which must remain unsaid. So far, we have confined our chat to passenger trains, but there is another all-important side of railway working, namely, that of the freight train services : the trains upon which we all depend for the distribution of raw materials and of manufactured goods. You may not be aware that, although the passenger services are more in public prominence, it is the mineral and merchandise trains which earn a very large part of the revenue of the railways.

The general public know less of this side of railway activity, for many of the freight trains travel in the night hours. A visit to a large goods station at night or in the early hours of the morning would probably be an " eye-opener " to many whose knowledge of railway working is confined to what may be observed in the hours of daylight.

It was Lord Bacon who said, " There are three things which make a nation great and prosperous : a fertile soil, busy workshops, and easy conveyance of men and commodities from place to place." Little reflection is necessary to realise how important is the third thing, the conveyance of commodities. The fertile soil and the busy workshops are both dependent upon the " means of conveyance " for the distribution of their products. It is the freight trains which constitute the bridge between the producers and the consumers.

The conveyance of merchandise appears to have been a matter of secondary consideration when railways were first constructed, and the earliest timebills in existence have no reference to goods train services at all. For some time progress in this direction seems to have been slow, but during the past twenty years there has been a speeding up in goods train working. The introduction of vacuum brake fitted goods stock, in which the Great Western Railway took the lead, marked an epoch in freight train services, and with the building of big engines specially designed for goods train haulage there has been a vast improvement in regard to these " trains that pass in the night."

From an average of about fifteen miles per hour, the speed of our freight trains has risen to something like forty-five miles per hour, whilst at the same time the loads have increased by nearly 100 per cent. Twice the load at three times the speed !

The Great Western Railway prides itself on having one of the finest express freight train services in the country. Four times a week the fastest goods train in the United Kingdom—and, it is believed, in the world—leaves London for the North of England and Scotland. Because it carries such household commodities as margarine, tea, coffee, and cocoa, it has been nicknamed " The Grocers' Express." Its speed is almost equal to that of an ordinary London-to-Scotland passenger train.

Starting on the Great Western Railway at Southall Station at 11.55 A.M., it goes on to Greenford, Middlesex; Princes Risborough, Buckinghamshire; Leamington, Warwickshire; Wolverhampton, Crewe, Glasgow, Edinburgh, and at about eight o'clock next morning goods are being unloaded from it in Aberdeen. The most direct London-Aberdeen route is over 522 miles.

Improvement in the rapid rail transport of merchandise has not been without its advantages to the traders of the country. Whereas in the old days it was the practice for the merchants to hold large stocks of goods, such stocks are now a thing of the past except, perhaps, in raw materials. The trader who orders his supplies by telephone or telegraph one day, can, relying upon fast freight train services, get delivery the following day, even though the goods have to be conveyed hundreds of miles. This, as you will readily understand, all means money in the traders' pockets, as less capital is locked up in stock and less storage accommodation has to be provided than was formerly the case.

CHAPTER THE SEVENTEENTH

RAILWAY GROUPING

There has been so much in the Press on the subject of late, that perhaps I ought not to omit some brief reference to the grouping of railways which has recently been carried out under the provisions of the Railways Act, 1921. This Act provides for the railways of the country, with a few exceptions, being divided into four main groups, of which the Great Western Railway is one.

It is interesting to note that the Great Western is the only railway which under the grouping maintains its name and identity. It has absorbed some thirty-two smaller railway companies, and the Greater Great Western Railway now embraces practically all the Welsh railways and also the whole of the railway-owned docks in South Wales, and is now the largest dock-owning company in the Kingdom. It spreads over about 8,000 miles of track, with about 1,500 stations and halts, and serves about 1,000 miles of coast line. The locomotives number over 3,900, passenger-train vehicles over 10,000, and the wagon stock is approaching the 100,000 figure.

The members of the staff of this undertaking number

approximately 110,000. You will better realise what this means when I tell you that, supposing they stood hand in hand in a single line along the permanent way beginning at Paddington, this human chain would reach beyond Birmingham and it would take an express train about two hours to pass it.

During the year 1922 the Great Western Railway carried 128,639,316 passengers, irrespective of season ticket holders (91,326). The total number of engine miles run was 86,309,020, or approximately the distance of the earth from the sun on January 1.

As has been said, under the grouping the Great Western Railway maintains the same name as heretofore. It also maintains the same policy, and "G.W.R." will still stand in the future, as it has done in the past, for the hallmark of efficiency in railway transport.

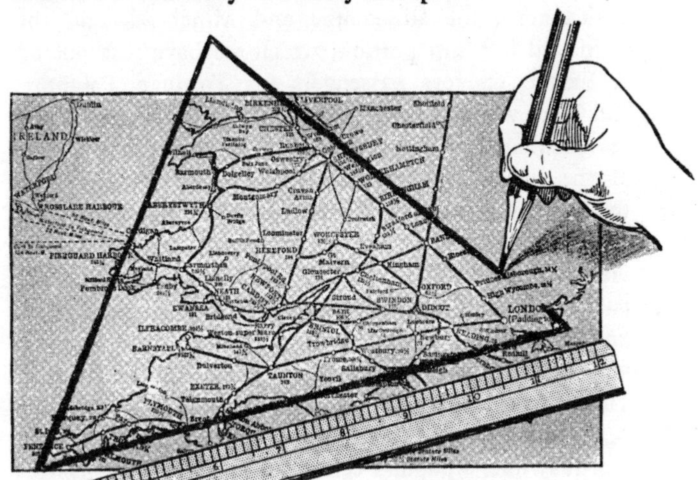

The G.W.R. Group in a Triangle

CHAPTER THE EIGHTEENTH

GLORIOUS DEVON

We are now in glorious Devon—"the Shire of the Sea Kings." The station we are passing is Exeter. It is barely 1.30 P.M., so we are running dead on time, for our slip portion is due at the station at half-past one precisely.

We have now detached the third of our slip portions—the first at Westbury, for the Weymouth line, the second at Taunton, for Ilfracombe and Minehead, and the third and last slip portion, which we have just put off at Exeter, conveys passengers for Torquay, Paignton, and Dartmouth. Here we get our first glimpse of the sea at what is a more than usually interesting section of the line. We practically run along by the coast, the railway having been blasted out of the rock. We pass through one or two short tunnels and get a good view of the beach at Dawlish and Teignmouth. The two rocks standing out so conspicuously in the sea are known as the "Parson and Clerk," and the long sea wall which is now on your left reaches practically from Dawlish to Teignmouth.

Passing Newton Abbot, which is the junction for the Torquay line, a popular centre for many of Devonshire's beauty spots, including Dartmoor, we speed on through Totnes, situated on the western bank of the River Dart, through some delightful and typical Devonshire country.

I really think I ought at this stage of our journey to grant you some brief respite in order to allow you to view the lovely country through which we are passing. Someone has spoken of Devon as "God's Garden," and it would indeed be almost a sacrilege not to give some little time to the admiration of our beautiful surroundings.

It was, I believe, Robert Louis Stevenson who said that the best way to see our lovely island was from the windows of a railway train. I think he must have expressed that opinion after "Going Great Western" through Devon. Don't you?

∽ ∽ ∽ ∽

We are rapidly approaching our destination and are, in effect, already on the outskirts of Plymouth. With Devonport and Stonehouse, Plymouth forms the "Three Towns" noted for military and naval establishments. Overlooking Plymouth Sound, an arm of the English Channel between Devonshire and Cornwall, is the Hoe, where the Armada and Drake monuments are situated, also Smeaton's Tower—the old Eddystone Lighthouse. West of the Hoe is Millbay with the Docks of the Great Western Railway. Plymouth has for centuries been famous for its men who "go down to the sea in ships." Memorable events connected with the port are the assembly of the fleet to oppose the Armada (1588), the departures of the Cadiz expedition (1596), and of the Pilgrim

Fathers (1620). As every schoolboy knows, it was from Plymouth that Frobisher, Gilbert, Drake, and Raleigh sailed on their adventurous voyages in the days of Good Queen Bess.

∽ ∽ ∽

Now we feel a gentle application of the vacuum brake and, gradually reducing our speed, we come to a stand at Plymouth North Road Station at 2.37 P.M., having completed our wonderful non-stop run of 226 miles in four hours and seven minutes to the very tick. Splendid !

Here we leave our train to continue its run over the Saltash Bridge and through sunny Cornwall to Penzance (305 miles from Paddington) where, after making one or two stops, it arrives at 5 o'clock—just six and a half hours after leaving London.

∽ ∽ ∽ ∽

We have travelled far in a few short hours, and during our journey I hope I have been able to enlighten you with regard to some of the more interesting aspects of railway working. Much has necessarily had to be left unsaid: some phases of railway activity but briefly mentioned, and many others omitted altogether.

Unfortunately it has not been possible to make more than a few references to the many points of interest *en route*. Had time permitted, you could have been told more of the many historic and other associations of the places through which we have passed.

From the knowledge you have gained, however, you will, I think, be able to realise what a wonderful thing a modern railway is, and particularly (note this, please) what a wonderful railway the Great Weſtern is. If I have enabled you to realise that, I have not altogether failed in my undertaking.

You will now be able to appreciate why so many thousands of travellers " Go Great Weſtern " when on business or pleasure bent—" They ' Go Great Weſtern ' because the going's good."

AU REVOIR

INDEX

INDEX